Christopher Lloyd

Edited by
Erica Hunningher

Photographs by
Jonathan Buckley

COLOUR
for
Adventurous
Gardeners

Half title page
Salvia involucrata *'Bethellii'* with Dahlia *'Chimborazo'*.

Title page
*The end of the Long Border at Great Dixter in early
August, with orange* Kniphofia uvaria *'Nobilis' and*
Helenium *'Moerheim Beauty', pink phlox, yellow
verbascum and purple* Clematis *'Jackmanii Superba' –
planted with plenty of soothing greens.*

Contents page
Densely packed flower heads of Verbena bonariensis.

Colour for Adventurous Gardeners
First published in hardback in 2001
First published in paperback in 2004
Text copyright © Christopher Lloyd 2001
The moral right of the author has been asserted

Photographs copyright © Jonathan Buckley 2001

ISBN 0 563 52171 6

Published by BBC Books, BBC Worldwide Ltd,
Woodlands, 80 Wood Lane, London W12 0TT

Conceived and edited by Erica Hunningher
Commissioning editor: Vivien Bowler
Designed and typeset in Scala by STUDIOGOSSETT

Printed and bound in Great Britain by
Butler & Tanner, Frome & London
Colour separations by Radstock Reproductions Ltd,
Midsomer Norton
Cover printed by Lawrence Allen Ltd,
Weston-super-Mare

For information about this
and other BBC books,
please visit our website on
www.bbcshop.com
or telephone 08700 777 001

COLOUR
for
Adventurous
Gardeners

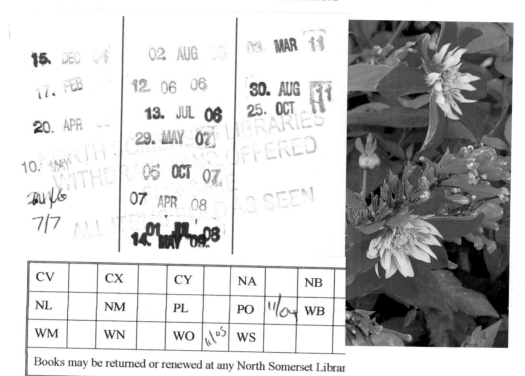

Please return/renew this item by the last date shown.

North Somerset
COUNCIL

CONTENTS

COLOUR Go for it!

The limitations imposed by rules are a safe haven, but the adventurous gardener will want to try something different.

◄ *A carefully managed field of cornfield 'weeds' at The Old Vicarage, East Ruston, near the Norfolk coast, in July. The mixture of primary colours is vastly satisfying. Buy seed of the various species individually and mix them yourself, omitting over-aggressive species like corncockle, although this is included in all ready-made mixtures.*

The field is cut in October. A month later, perennial weeds need to be treated with herbicide. When this has taken effect, the field is ploughed and harrowed. Mostly its contents will be perpetuated by self-seeding, but topping up can be practised of any desired species that is decreasing. The site must be entirely open.

The use of colour in gardens has become something of a cult subject. Hence the spate of books on it – at least five in the past fifteen years. Why should this be and can there be anything more to say? After all, the most important aspects of gardening are, first, to grow plants that you like and to grow them well. Next, to have a firm and cooperative structure to the garden in which they are to be grown. Then, to work out the seasons of display during which you want your plantings to be effective so they make intense use of the site and never become boring; this will involve organizing successions, so that one plant is there to take over from another, as needed. Then we must recognize the importance of structural plants so that we can compose a cohesive picture, and of foliage even more than of flowers, since foliage is longer on the scene and is generally bolder.

Plants that are grown close to one another need to be able to help each other, visually. For instance, one that creates a haze of small, variegated leaves needs either to have an interesting structure as a plant, by way of compensation – this is obtained by the tiered habit of *Cornus alternifolia* 'Argentea'; or to have neighbours or a backdrop with more sombre, perhaps bolder and contrasting foliage, rather than other small-leaved, variegated plants, which, carried to extremes, will produce the chaotic dog's-dinner effect. Leaf textures are an important consideration, and

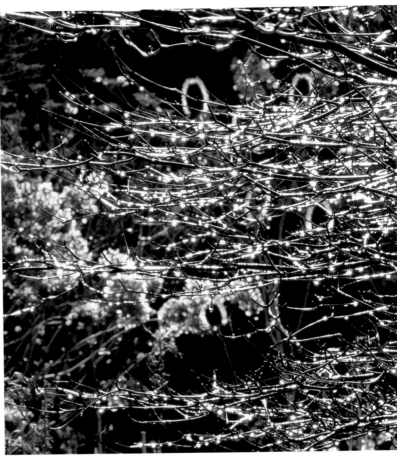

▲ Cornus alternifolia
'Argentea' in spring, with
self-sown forget-me-nots
underneath. The airy
foliage variegation is made
by quite tiny leaves but the
shrub's strong structure
with horizontal branching
saves it from being an
amorphous haze.

whether their surfaces are matt and light absorbing or glossy and light reflecting.

Then, at last, we reach colour, but as can now be seen, it is not an end in itself. Yet it is a side to gardening that gets many gardeners worried. Choice of colour is so wide that they deliberately straitjacket themselves by developing prejudices against certain colours ('I hate orange') or in favour of others ('really, I should like my garden to be nothing but blue'). There are so many necessary restrictions in our lives that it seems a shame to impose more of them. For a broad understanding of our subject, I think we should recognize that all colours are potentially good but that certain expressions of a colour may be bad, like a muddy magenta or a mawkish salmon. This recognition gives us plenty of scope for picking and choosing.

Now to colour juxtapositions and here we're getting near the bone. Most popular are colour harmonies or, as has more recently become a vogue phrase, colour theming. Say we have a purple-

▲ The same cornus in winter. It is naked but as interesting as at other seasons, the branches purple. As they are horizontal, raindrops remain suspended in rows along the undersides, catching and reflecting the light.

▲▶ The apricot-orange dahlia, 'David Howard', is an important long-flowering feature in the Exotic Garden. It contrasts happily with airy mauve Verbena bonariensis and with dark Canna indica 'Purpurea' foliage.

flowered plant that we like; we think, what can I put next to that? Orange? Oh dear no; the Joneses would be terribly shocked at anything so blatant. Colour-anxious gardeners are always looking over their shoulders in fear of disapproval. Mauve, then? Yeees, but I don't really like mauve. How about lavender or lilac (meaning the colour rather than the flower)? Yes, that sounds nice.

So we trot around the garden to find a lilac- or lavender-coloured flower that's out now and that will go with our tall, deep mauve *Verbena bonariensis*. And we find *Thalictrum delavayi*, a haze of tiny mauve flowers but pining on its own. So we put them together. Voilà! And the Joneses congratulate us on our good taste, so we carry it a bit further, aiming perhaps at a purple border in the manner of the one at Sissinghurst Castle.

There is absolutely nothing wrong with all that, apart from subservience to the acknowledged superiority of the Joneses' views on taste. You should always listen to criticism, however. It may have a point. And never hesitate to put your critic on the spot

▶ This central section of the Long Border starts to be lively in April, with 'White Triumphator' tulips planted among foxgloves and surrounded by the border's overall spring theme of forget-me-nots.

◀ By early June, the foxgloves, Digitalis purpurea 'Sutton's Apricot' (later to be replaced by late-sown annuals), are in full bloom. The large mauve globes of self-sowing Allium cristophii are important in this area.

▶ Late June, with spires of Delphinium 'Mighty Atom'; contrasting flat heads of Achillea 'Lucky Break' in front; Geranium 'Ann Folkard' beside that; the frothy white Ammi majus behind. (This photograph is reproduced, enlarged, on pages 88-9.)

▲ By mid-August, the teazels are already browning but keep their structure till spring. Achillea 'Lucky Break' still performs. Cardoons are flowering at the back and the striking white bunheads of Hydrangea arborescens 'Annabelle' are in full blow.

▶ Last day of August. Allium cristophii and Achillea 'Lucky Break' have kept their shapes and Hydrangea arborescens 'Annabelle' will be a feature for months yet. So will the cardoons at the back.

by asking why? or why not? We may get fed up with children who are forever asking why, but it is really excellent and essential that they should be curious and enquiring. So, weigh up what the Joneses have to say and then decide for yourself.

I often practise colour harmonies myself. But just consider what you may be missing if you stick *only* in that groove. Think, for instance, of the apricot-orange-flowered, dark-leaved small decorative dahlia, 'David Howard' with your *V. bonariensis*. There you will have a strong contrast not only in colour but also in form, the bold and solid as against the light, see-through verbena.

That could increase your pulse rate by a beat or two and I do believe that excitement is an essential element in the most successful gardening. To put similar flower and foliage colours together is easy and it is always safe. Nothing is going to jar. To contrast them is more difficult. The field is wide open. Contrast them with what? Contrast is everywhere and could lead to chaos; where do I start?

Experiment is another of gardening's excitements. Try it out and see. Discuss the results with an open-minded friend and decide how far your experiment has been successful and in what manner it could be improved. Go on from there, always using plants that you really do like. Something will result, you may be sure, and it will be your own baby.

Violent contrasts will sometimes work against all the odds, depending on the light and the time of day, on the time of year and on our own mood. As we emerge from the drabness of winter, we yearn for colour and almost anything goes so long as we can sate ourselves with it. You may, in February, have a huge bush of *Daphne mezereum*, wreathed along all its branches with mauve-pink blossom; and underneath, a carpet of brilliant orange *Crocus* x *luteus*, open to the warmth of the sun. How could you resist being gladdened? The two colours may be shouting at each other, but they are shouting for joy.

You will sometimes (especially in Scotland in summer) see a small front garden that is literally packed with every colour under the sun, except, most likely, for grey (plenty of grey skies without that). It is wholly undigested and yet it is exuberant; it is full of joy, and that's a feeling that immediately communicates. 'What fun they've had!' you exclaim, even though you cannot approve the result. Probably the ingredients are all usable by yourself but, for one thing, you need larger patches as well as dots. Then you need quieter plants to set off the bright. But out-and-out disapproval of

▲ Glaucium corniculatum *is closely related to our native horned poppy,* G. flavum, *of sea coasts, but is orange with a yellow base, instead of yellow all through. It has glaucous, wavy-margined foliage and a long season, exhausted after a couple of years.*

▼ *A very different poppy,* Meconopsis x sheldonii. *The central boss of yellow stamens provides an excellent contrast to blue flowers which face outwards (see page 67). If there is some mauve in the blue petals, that is no detriment.*

that psychedelic garden, a closing of the eyes while turning your head aside and whispering 'oh dear!', is merely to expose your priggishness and how you have missed out on the gutsy side of gardening.

Given the right circumstances, I believe that every colour can be successfully used with any other and that is the message I hope to convey. It is not an approach that has so far been attempted, although Andrew Lawson's *The Gardener's Book of Colour* comes implicitly very near to it. There is something called the Colour Wheel that I have never understood and that I shall not therefore attempt to explore or explain. It is somehow intended to demonstrate which colours may successfully be put together and which may not, but the outcome makes no sense to me, so I shall go my own way without.

Rules, it has been said, are made to be broken. If there are rules, for instance in harmony when learning to write your own music, it is probably a good thing to know and understand them, but not to be content to leave the matter there. Bach knew all the rules but broke them whenever he needed to, and that is what makes his music so constantly unexpected and enthralling, even two and a half centuries later. Gertrude Jekyll, in our own field, is always being quoted and supposedly imitated – I shall quote her in due course to serve my own ends, for she was not hidebound by rules, which was what made her a supreme artist.

Not everyone has the gift of true originality but we can at least free ourselves of the unnecessary shackles imposed by convention. Go for it, would be my motto.

▲ *There are striking colour contrasts in the same flower as it ages, red to yellow to white, in this charming annual climber,* Ipomoea lobata *(syn.* Mina lobata). *Its host, here, is deep-mauve-flowered* Verbena bonariensis.

▼ Primula vialii *is hard to recognize as a primula apart from its primrose-like leaves. In bud, the flowers show their red sepals, but these are masked once the mauve corolla opens. Half-opened flower spikes are rather amazing.*

▶ *One of my favourite tulips, the Lily-flowered 'Queen of Sheba'. The flowers open in sunshine but wider still as the bloom ages, revealing a murky greenish-black centre. Quite an essay in contrasts.*

RED Nothing to Fear

Start with passion. We see red. We blush red with shame, embarrassed pleasure or anger. We wave a red rag at a bull to stir up its aggro. Red for danger. Red flowers, as also white, are not allowed in hospitals. Blood and bandages.

Thus warned and thoroughly inhibited, how shall we react to red flowers in our gardens? I just wish there was a greater range of choice. Few hardy perennials are truly red-flowered and we need to turn to the tender kinds and to annuals for further sustenance.

I don't want to hive all my reds into a ghetto, which is the cowardly treatment of a colour that, basically, you fear. 'Let's get it over,' is the implication, 'and then we shall be free to concentrate on the soft harmonies with which we feel safe and comfortable.' But red should mean excitement of the most exhilarating kind. What could be more stirring than an oriental poppy, newly opened and bursting into the sunrise of another blue day? To avoid growing red flowers because the colour is difficult is as tragic as wanting to be middle-aged before you have savoured the elixir of being young, adventurous and carefree.

So, how to use it? Red seems to have its own volcanic energy. It becomes electrifyingly intense towards sunset, then suddenly turns black, which is also exciting. So plant red flowers where they will catch the evening sun. They will combine well with many colours. Purple is excellent. I always think that the Purple Border at Sissinghurst only truly comes to life when two large specimens of *Rosa moyesii*, which were there before the purple theme was instituted but were allowed to remain, ripen their scarlet hips in August.

◄ Crocosmia *'Lucifer'* puts adrenalin into the midsummer scene but does have a rather short (July) season. Later, the seed heads are attractive. We need more red-flowered hardy perennials.

▲▲ *The tomato-red hips of* Rosa rugosa *start colouring in late summer and often overlap its own late flowers, which may be pink or magenta.*

▲ *Scarlet oriental poppies combine flamboyance with great delicacy of texture and deserve to be peered at (and photographed) close-up.*

Another dashing use of scarlet hips that I discovered by accident but am trading on (much of the best gardening evolves like this), sees the swags of ripe fruit on my sweet briars, *Rosa rubiginosa*, against the glistening, newly expanded cream-white plumes of pampas grass, *Cortaderia selloana* 'Pumila', in early fall.

You might think that scarlet and pink was beyond the pale, but nature often defies good taste. The Rugosa rose, 'Fru Dagmar Hastrup' (2m/7ft), which makes an excellent hedge, has single pink flowers which are quickly followed by tomato-red hips. Fruits are ripe in late summer but flowering continues way beyond that. The two together, admittedly mitigated by abundance of healthy foliage, are great. Later, the foliage changes to lemon yellow, so that the combination becomes yellow and red. Welcome to that, too.

To return to our oriental poppies. They flower quite early and it is easiest to combine them with the green foliage of as yet unflowering perennials. The whole scene comes to life. Red with grey is good too, as when the blood red, upstanding poppy 'Goliath' is grown in front of the jagged grey-green young foliage of cardoons, *Cynara cardunculus*. Get the poppies well in front, as the cardoon develops a wide spread. A purple and red combination that I enjoy is where I have the typical scarlet oriental in front of the young shoots of *Clematis recta* 'Purpurea' (illustrated on page 160). The latter will presently need massive support, but I manage to delay providing this until the poppies have had their say.

The annual ladybird poppy (ladybug, to Americans), *Papaver commutatum*, is of a deep crimson colouring, with a large black blotch at the base of each petal – red and black is smart. In a sort of cottage-garden context, we have threaded that between and among a carmine pink, biennial cranesbill, *Geranium rubescens*, which self-sows abundantly. There is much else going on, including self-sown blue forget-me-nots. The effect is fresh and lively. On another occasion we raised the poppy from spring-sown seed, planting it out from individual pots in swathes around discrete clumps (perhaps 1m/40in apart) of *Sanguisorba tenuifolia* 'Alba'. That, at 90cm/36in, is twice the poppy's height and it has arching brushes of white blossom. Another excellent red and white team has ladybird poppies (crimson and black) with white Canterbury bells. (It always helps to prolong the Canterbury's season and smarten the scene up, if you dead-head its spent, brown blooms every third day.)

Large blocks of undiluted red are a mistake; indigestible as swallowing a lump of uncooked dough. You see this especially in spring, with red rhododendrons or evergreen azaleas, in which there is so much blossom that not a leaf is to be seen. This makes you blink, which is no bad thing, but then you long for some supporting cast; nothing around can compete. It is the same with the municipal bedder's fall-back: scarlet salvias with blood-curdling names like 'Blaze of Fire', 'Bonfire', 'Firecracker', 'Fury', 'Inferno', 'Red River', 'Sizzler Red' and 'Volcano'.

In these salvias, both the corolla and the calyx are scarlet. By the time the breeders have dwarfened them into compact, featureless nonentities, there is nothing but scarlet to be seen.

▲ *The rich crimson oriental poppy 'Goliath', here contrasted with a bright yellow, giant buttercup, Ranunculus acris 'Stevenii'. I must have my bit of fun. The grass, Stipa gigantea, is an emollient.*

▶▶ *Discrete clumps of the fluffy white perennial* Sanguisorba tenuifolia 'Alba' *are interplanted for midsummer effect with a carpet of the ladybird poppy,* Papaver commutatum. *It will later be replaced with a bedding plant for late summer and autumn.*

▲ *The bedding-out annual salvia,* S. coccinea *'Lady in Red', contrasts strikingly in many contexts, which can be easily varied from year to year or even within the same year. Here seen with the purplish annual,* Browallia americana; Centaurea gymnocarpa *(now changed to* C. cineraria) *in front.*

▶ *The protagonist either side of* Salvia coccinea *'Lady in Red', at a border's margin, is blue lyme grass,* Leymus arenarius. *Behind red-flowered cannas, whose bold leaves are a great asset, the red fruits of* Rosa setipoda *and* Viburnum opulus *'Compactum'.*

This may be a triumph of a kind but it is monotonous and is not improved by combining it with equally dumpy and featureless double orange marigolds. However, *Salvia coccinea*, which is by nature a rather too rangy and small-flowered species for garden effect, has been vastly improved in 'Lady in Red', which is shorter (45cm/18in), though not uncomfortably short, with more flower power while remaining a decently free, self-respecting plant. In my garden I like it interplanted with the bright purple *Verbena rigida* (38cm/15in), sown in early March. It also makes an excellent surround to blue lyme grass, *Leymus arenarius* (60cm/24in), grown entirely for its gracefully arching blue leaves.

That red can combine and contrast well with other strong colours is shown in mixtures of bedding-out impatiens. There you see red with bright pink, magenta, strong purple, orange and white. The wonder is that it works, but it does. I should add, however, that a position beneath the dappled shade of trees is necessary, to avoid being blinded, and that it is a great help if the impatiens strain used is not so dwarfened as to eliminate the mitigating influence of dark green leaves and a relaxed habit.

▲ Red bedding 'geraniums' fill the gaps between the lowest glaucous sword-leaves of Furcraea longaeva. *The paddle-shaped leaves of Canna 'Durban' (known as 'Tropicanna' in many countries) contribute contrast. This all peaks in late summer.*

◄ *Mid-August in the Exotic Garden with Dahlia 'Grenadier' contrasting with the garden's main theme plant, the self-sowing, purple* Verbena bonariensis. Canna indica 'Purpurea' *adds further emphasis.*

Unfortunately the breeders do not agree, the dwarfer the better being their aim.

Among my favourite tender perennials are dahlias and cannas. Both combine well with each other but also with other mixed plantings. Both have a range of powerful manifestations.

An advantage in many red-flowered cannas is the extra weight and emphasis given by their purple-bronze leaves. *Canna indica* 'Purpurea' is vigorous to 1.8m/6ft or more. Its light red flowers are quite small, yet appropriate and I do not go along with some of my colleagues who prefer to prevent it from flowering and to treat it entirely as a foliage plant. It looks twice itself if grown next to second-year seedlings of the gum, *Eucalyptus gunnii*. This will be in its juvenile state (2.4m/8ft), with quite small, rounded leaves of metallic glaucous colouring. (If it survives the winter, rejuvenate with a hard cut-back in spring.)

It is nice to use colour harmonies as well as contrasts, especially if the plants themselves are entirely different in respects other than colour. A good team, in my experience, is of *Viburnum opulus* 'Compactum' (1.5m/5ft) behind or beside the same canna. This viburnum is the guelder rose (Guelderland, in the

Netherlands, is one of its native habitats). It has rather maple-like, palmate leaves and white lacecap flowers in May, which are an asset in themselves. Then, in August, its dangling clusters of shining red berries are already ripe and they hang on for many weeks, totally disregarded by birds. Such is my experience, anyway. So this is excellent in a mixed border beside the tall purple-leaved canna or behind the slightly shorter C. 'General Eisenhower' (there is some doubt about this name). This canna's broad, bronze leaves take on beautiful curves, like a piece of sculpture, and are crowned by large, intense red flowers. It scarcely tops 1.8m/6ft and may well be less, which suits the way I grow and prune the viburnum (by the removal, in winter, of all its flowered wood, leaving the straight, unbranched new wood intact to carry the next season's crop). The shrub's height can largely be

◄▲ *The Exotic Garden in August, seen through a screen of the sumptuous Small Semi-cactus dahlia, D. 'Wittemans Superba' (red with a hint of purple on the reverse side of its rays) and* Verbena bonariensis.

▲ *Red contrasts with particular effect against purple and glaucous foliage. Here,* Dahlia *'Alva's Doris',* Canna indica *'Purpurea' and the juvenile foliage of seedling* Eucalyptus gunnii, *which is hardy.*

◄ Dahlia *'Bishop of Llandaff'. Popular even with non-lovers of dahlias, because of its contrasting, deeply cut purple foliage.*

controlled by the way you prune it.

If the leaves of most dahlias are a trifle mundane, don't be put off by that. The failing is easily masked by companion plants of a different kind and also by its own flowers, which rise above the foliage. There is at least one notable dahlia, however, famed for its foliage, which is purple and deeply dissected. This is 'Bishop of Llandaff', and its semi-single flowers are pure red. There is considerable snobbery about dahlias (growing weaker, I hope), which dismisses them as vulgar, on the basis of the coarse growth and enormous, prize-winning blooms of the class known as giant decs (Giant Decoratives). These are scarcely for garden use at all, but the majority of dahlias have neat blooms in a variety of shapes.

Dahlia 'Bishop of Llandaff' (1.2m/4ft) will reach 1.8m/6ft if given a long season to grow in and is a splendid companion for

25

▼ Fascicularia bicolor *is unusual and surprisingly hardy. It makes low cushions of spine-edged leaves, borne in rosettes. When about to flower, late summer or autumn, the central leaves change to red and surround a cushion of baby-blue flowers. Can you resist such a plant?*

▲ *The flame nasturtium, Tropaeolum speciosum, looks best growing over an evergreen hedge. The tropaeolum is herbaceous (it dislikes lime), so the support is given a breather in winter and can be trimmed then.*

tall, deep mauve *Verbena bonariensis*. This is a see-through plant, more stem than leaf, a short-lived perennial with a prodigiously long flowering season from late June to late October. In warm-temperate climates it is a common weed of cultivation, self-sowing abundantly, which may put some gardeners off it. If they garden in Scotland or Vermont, by contrast, no seed will be set and the plants will die out unless the precaution is taken of propagating them from cuttings.

If you propagate dahlias from cuttings, late, say in early May, their flowering will be entirely fresh in October (frosts permitting). I half accidentally found myself with a pleasing contrast where the Bishop (only 1m/40in high because of its late start) was planted near to *Nerine bowdenii*, which has heads of bright pink trumpets, and a shrub-cherry, *Prunus glandulosa* 'Alba Plena'. This last has wands of double white blossom in April, after which it is pruned hard back all over to restrict its height to 1.2m/4ft. The foliage on the young wands thus resulting changes to soft peachy pink in autumn. So there you have it: a red-flowered tender perennial, a bright pink-flowered bulb and a gentle pink-leaved shrub. Not forgetting golden autumn sunshine after sparkling dew, as accompaniments.

If you happen to live in a frost pocket, that's too bad, but most of us should, I think, give more thought to the autumn garden, when there is so much residual warmth to enjoy. 'Ellen Huston' (75cm/30in) is another dahlia good for that season, rather on the orange side of red, semi-double blooms and a compact habit suited to bedding. Its leaves are quite bronzed. It flowers earlier, by the beginning of July, but most strongly quite late. 'Grenadier' (1.2m/4ft), is a small, fully double, strong red decorative dahlia that also gives me much pleasure. With normal treatment and from overwintered tubers, it is one of the first to flower, in early July, but late-struck cuttings will behave in the way I have just described, peaking in October.

If you do live where early frosts are to be expected, advantage can be taken of the situation by growing certain trees and shrubs notable for flaring up in fall. Few, if any, of these are native to Britain and we depend mainly on Japan and North America for species, like the scarlet oak, *Quercus coccinea*, that are normally ready to oblige in this way, but are always best when a timely frost has occurred a week or so before the leaves turn.

As with rhododendron blossom in spring and *Salvia splendens* in summer, solid blocks of autumnal red, albeit exciting, are far

▲ Grevillea 'Canberra Gem' is a pretty hardy shrub with fresh green needle leaves making a cheerful background to its blossom. This is borne in succession for at least four spring months.

▼ An ideal contrast for the vine, Vitis coignetiae, in its prolonged crimson red autumn season, is a wild ivy, Hedera helix, with glossy, rich evergreen foliage. They are growing up an ash tree. Plenty of moisture at the root is essential for the vine.

from subtle and will look the better for being set off by rich greenery. The rowan, *Sorbus scalaris* (10m/30ft), succeeds in this all on its own. Its clusters of crimson berries ripen while the surrounding foliage is still intense green. Again to the point, as leaves change from green to red, they will pass through a stage when residual green remains along the leaf veins. This is even more attractive than when the entire leaf has turned to uniform red.

Autumn tints do not just depend on species and weather in the run-up. Some clones will be much readier to colour brilliantly than others. When these are vegetatively propagated, they are given cultivar names, as *Quercus coccinea* 'Splendens'. It will be more expensive, because of having needed to be grafted, whereas a seed-raised plant is far cheaper to produce, but its dependability will be well worth the extra money.

Possibly the most ornamental of all the true vines is *Vitis coignetiae*, because of its extra-large leaves and a vigorous habit which allows it to fling long swags of foliage over its support. This Japanese species colours to a beautiful crimson-red and never looks better than against the lustrous green background of common ivy, say growing up an ash, which is a tree with a thinnish, light-admitting crown and therefore particularly suited to being climbed over.

The vine has an abnormally long season of high colouring – perhaps up to six weeks. Two warnings to avoid disappointment. Some clones will go year after year without colouring well at all. If you cannot easily come by a named clone, like Claret Cloak ('Frovit'), of proven performance, visit a nursery or garden centre in autumn and examine their stock, which will be pot grown. Now, a pot-grown plant may, due to semi-starvation at the root, be readier to colour up than it would in the open ground, but generally a highly coloured vine offered for sale is likely to be capable of a similar performance in your garden.

The other warning is to ensure that your plant is not interred in poor, dry, dusty, root-infested soil. It will never take off. Prepare a really good position with plenty of bulky organic matter included, at the start. Plant well forward from the tree to be climbed over, where roots are less of a problem, apply annual surface mulches but also water heavily during the plant's growing season. Of course you can plant over a high fence or on a quarry face or some other inert support, but a supporting tree will look best.

Among the most exciting undiluted red flowers are hybrids derived from the North American *Lobelia cardinalis* and *L. fulgens*.

▲ *A satisfying tapestry effect in damp shade with Lobelia F₁ 'Fan Scharlach', the green whorls of Paris polyphylla and variegated periwinkle. Lobelias in the F₁ Fan Series have a tall, central spike but branch freely to make a bush of blossom, from August to October.*

'Queen Victoria' has upright spires, to 1m/3ft, above purple foliage. It looks super with a background of the green-and-white-striped (more white than green, in the most desirable strains) grass, *Arundo donax* var. *versicolor*. Most of us must treat these two as tender perennials for summer bedding. Among recent seed strains I am greatly impressed by F$_I$ Fan Scarlet ('Fan Scharlach'). Seedlings vary in colour a little (it is easy to select and retain the best for subsequent years) but are generally bright, pure red and the plant's habit is bushy, to 75cm/30in, not skinny, as 'Queen Victoria' is inclined to be. Fan Scarlet can be treated as a half-hardy annual but the thrifty gardener will lift stock at the end of the season and bed it in under glass, where little frost will enter. Then split and make more of the crowns of dormant shoots in spring. Fan Deep Red ('Fan Tiefrot') is also good, but the scarlet strain shows up the better in a garden setting.

▲ A robust perennial for some gardeners (but not with me), the 90cm/36in *Lobelia tupa flowers in summer and is hardy in this coastal garden, The Old Vicarage, East Ruston, Norfolk.*

▶▲ *An old herbaceous border stalwart,* Lychnis chalcedonica, *carries its heads (some 7.5cm/3in across) of pure scarlet flowers for all too few weeks at midsummer. The stiff, rough stems become top-heavy after rain, swaying over from the base, and need to be supported.*

Of pure, red-flowered hardy perennials, *Lychnis chalcedonica* (90cm/36in) is an old cottage-garden favourite, with domes of scarlet flowers, each petal notched, giving it the pet name of Maltese cross. However, nitpickers will point out that there are five petals, not four. Its domed heads in early July contrast well in every way with the purple spikes of *Salvia* x *superba*, which is equally hardy, but has a far longer season than the lychnis's three weeks.

Every bit as pure and punchy a red is that of *Lychnis* x *haageana* (30cm/12in). This is a short-lived perennial which we find most satisfactorily treated as biennial, sowing the seed in July, bringing the seedlings on in individual plugs, then into 8cm/3^1/$_2$in pots, overwintered in a cold frame and planted out in spring. They will flower at the same time as Canterbury bells, which are twice their height but no matter. You can interplant the campanulas with the

29

◄ My own seedling, Crocosmia 'Late Lucifer', from 'Lucifer' itself, flowers usefully about two weeks later. Here seen backed by Catalpa bignonioides 'Aurea', treated as a shrub by hard annual pruning. An interlarding of annual orach, Atriplex hortensis var. rubra, with purple leaves. A great self-sower.

► The same crocosmia as on the opposite page but looking towards Phlox paniculata 'Alba', Kniphofia uvaria 'Nobilis' (the poker, just starting) and Eupatorium purpureum. These are all in a nursery stock bed, where we plant in groups, rather than in rows and have a lot more fun that way.

► Crocosmia masoniorum 'Dixter Flame' (my seedling) hanging over a colony of the aggressively spreading Houttuynia cordata 'Chameleon'. We enclose the roots of this with upright iron sheets, to stop its progress, but it is a nice-looking plant.

31

lychnis and the latter's scarlet colouring on a flower twice the size of *L. chalcedonica* is so dominant that it easily makes the desired impact, June-July being the height of this combined season. A mixture of blue, purple and white Canterburys will be ideal but we were surprised to find that even when some pink bells were in the mixture they by no means spoiled the effect. The Canterburys being biennial, the whole planting could be swept aside in early August and replaced with further bedding to finish off the season.

Moderately hardy are some of the red-flowered *Crocosmia*, notably the tall (1.2m/4ft), robust 'Lucifer'. This flowers in late July and only for three weeks. It looks well with acid lime-green, as all pure reds do. For instance the annual *Bupleurum falcatum*. But I get a thrill when it has *Lychnis coronaria*, often self-sown, growing up and into it from a group's margin. The lychnis is a dashing shade of magenta, slightly toned down by the plant's grey stems and calyx. It seems always to be on the lookout for new habitats and will give you numerous surprises.

Talking of lime-green and red, a sure-fire success in spring combines the single red *Anemone* x *fulgens* (23cm/9in) with a lowish euphorbia, like *E. myrsinites*, which keeps very low, *E. rigida* (30cm/12in) or even *E. polychroma* (30cm/12in when flowering but taller later). My aim with the last two (only I cannot quite get the anemone going) is to have them in front of the shrubby *Euphorbia* x *martinii* (60cm/24in), which is green with red central dots, and two Lily-flowered tulips: 'Dyanito', which is pure scarlet, and 'Ballerina', which is orange. All these are very lively in the spring garden.

In the middle of writing this, on a chilly, mid-January day, I looked out of my north window near sunset to see everything that could be reached bathed in warm sunlight. I had to hurry outside to enjoy it. At the top of my long border, the best feature year-round is a tall cone of the holly, *Ilex* x *altaclerensis* 'Golden King', which has relatively prickle-free leaves, broadly margined in yellow. Against the odds, one would say, it is a female and it berries regularly – this year not especially heavily, but they were still there, the birds not having been under climatic pressure. By day, I hardly notice them, but at this moment and in this light, every little cluster was picked out and highlighted in its green and yellow background. To say that this was magical may sound banal, but it was that and it was the colour red which was the magician.

▲ *The Darwin hybrid tulip, 'Red Matador', has persisted in the same position in my Long Border for thirty years, clumping up generously. It flowers quite early and sunshine opens the blooms to reveal their wonderful interiors.*

▶ *Contrast in Beth Chatto's gravel garden in April, with the scarlet Anemone x fulgens among low-growing Euphorbia myrsinites whose grey-blue leaves are barely visible beneath its lime-green, wide-spreading flower heads.*

▼ *Red and orange contrast effectively with the acid lime-green of euphorbias, here the shrubby* Euphorbia x martinii. *The orange tulip is 'Ballerina'; the red one 'Dyanito'. Both are Lily-flowered.*

Anemone x **fulgens**
Flame anemone
Height: 23cm /9in
Spread: 15cm/6in
Hardy, sun
A tuberous anemone bearing vivid saucer-shaped, scarlet flowers in spring. The red is enhanced by the black boss of stamens in the centre of the flower. Try with lime-green plants, such as low-growing *Euphorbia myrsinites*, which likes the same moderately fertile, light, well-drained soil.
◀

Canna indica 'Purpurea'
Indian shot
Height: 2m/6ft
Spread: 50cm/24in
Tender, sun
One of the most robust, purple-leaved cannas, with red flowers typically bunched like silk handkerchiefs at the crown of tall stems. 'General Eisenhower' is slightly shorter. Lift and store the rhizomes in just-moist soil, in a cool but frost-free spot over winter. Plant against the young, grey foliage of *Eucalyptus gunnii*.

Crocosmia 'Lucifer'
Montbretia
Height: 1.2m/4ft
Spread: 30cm/12in
Hardy, sun
Handsomely ridged foliage and floating, upward-facing flowers of the most brilliant red in high summer. For daring contrast, allow magenta *Lychnis coronaria* to seed itself around a colony; for less contrast try it with *Bupleurum falcatum*.

Dahlia 'Grenadier' ▲
Height: 1.2m/4ft
Spread: 45cm/18in
Tender, sun
A small, open-centred decorative bearing small, double, rich red flowers with reflexed rays, in July from stored tubers, in late autumn from cuttings. It mixes well with the autumn golds, such as *Rudbeckia* 'Goldsturm', or the blues such as *Aster* x *frikartii*. *D.* 'Ellen Huston' is more compact. *D.* 'Bishop of Llandaff', looks good amongst purple-leaved cannas and interwoven with *Verbena bonariensis*.

Ilex x **altaclerensis** 'Golden King'
Holly
Height: 6m/20ft
Spread: 5m /16ft
Hardy, sun or light shade
A virtually prickle-free holly with bright red berries and foliage broadly margined in yellow, a feature at every season. Plant with a red Viticella clematis threaded through its branches.

Impatiens
Height: 60cm/24in
Spread: 60cm/24in
Tender, sun or light shade
Named or unnamed cultivars offered as bedding and container plants provide varying shades of red. Mix with other coloured forms. Choose dark foliage and avoid over-dwarfed strains.

Lobelia F$_1$ 'Fan Scharlach'
Height: 75cm /30in
Spread: 23cm/9in
Tender, sun or partial shade.
A bushy perennial with bright red flowers, often grown from seed each year. It can be overwintered in a cold frame or treated as an annual. Try it with mid- to bright-green plants such as *Paris polyphylla*.
▼

Lobelia 'Queen Victoria'
Height: 90cm/36in
Spread: 30cm/12in
Marginally hardy, sun
Spires of bright red flowers above purple foliage. In frosty areas it is best treated as a bedding plant. Overwinter in a cold frame and split the crowns in the following spring. It looks good beside water or in front of the tall green and white grass *Arundo donax* var. *versicolor*.

Lychnis chalcedonica
Maltese cross
Height: 90cm/36in
Spread: 30cm/12in
Hardy, sun
Domed heads of bright scarlet flowers on stems that tend to blow sideways. Easily increased by division or from seed. It goes well with strong yellows. For a greater contrast, try it with purple *Salvia* x *superba*.

Lychnis x **haageana**
Height: 30cm/12in
Spread: 30cm/12in
Sun
A short-lived perennial, best treated as a biennial, with bright red or orange flowers up to 5cm/2in across, each of the five petals being notched. Plant with Canterbury bells, either in their white form or a mixture of colours, or with rambling *Petunia integrifolia*.

Meconopsis punicea
Poppy
Height: 30cm/12in
Spread: 30cm/12in
Partial shade
Just about the only pure red Meconopsis and of difficult cultivation, best in Scotland. Moist, acid soil and cool, partially shaded conditions. It frequently flowers itself to death. Raise new batches from seed. Success will make your reputation.

Papaver commutatum 'Ladybird'
Ladybird poppy
Height: 45cm/18in
Spread: 15cm/6in
Hardy annual, sun
Each bright crimson petal has a large black spot at the base, making a smart contrast with white *Campanula medium* and livening up pink and purple companions, such as *Geranium rubescens*. Grow from seed each year.

Papaver orientale 'Goliath Group'
Oriental poppy
Height: 90cm/3ft
Spread: 75cm/30in
Hardy, sun
A spectacular oriental poppy with dinner-plate-sized flowers of brilliant red in early summer. For a clash of the giants, place with the magenta *Geranium psilostemon* or in front of the silver-leaved *Cynara cardunculus*.

Penstemon 'Chester Scarlet'
Height: 60cm/24in
Spread: 30cm/12in
Hardy, sun or partial shade
Showy and as near to pure red as you'll find. Take cuttings as a precaution, as it is not that long-lived. Try with white *Lilium candidum*, which also prefers neutral to alkaline soil.

Quercus coccinea
Scarlet oak
Height: 20m/70ft
Spread: 15m/50ft
Hardy, sun or light shade
A green-leaved oak tree that turns a brilliant red in the autumn, all the more so if this is preceded by a frost. Some forms colour better than others and named ones such as 'Splendens' are likely to be reliable. Its ultimate size rules it out for the small garden.

Rosa 'Fru Dagmar Hastrup'
Rugosa rose
Height: 2m/7ft
Spread: 2m/7ft
Hardy, sun or part shade
Produces large red hips in late summer which go well with the remaining single, pink flowers and, later, with the yellow autumn leaves. Makes a good informal hedge as well as a specimen plant. Can be horribly chlorotic on lime.

Salvia coccinea 'Lady in Red'
Height: 45cm/18in
Spread: 30cm/12in
Tender, sun
A perennial treated as an annual. Loose spikes of bright red flowers, appearing over dark green leaves for most of the summer and autumn, make a good contrast with the bright purple *Verbena rigida*. A sympathetic planting is with the blue lyme grass, *Leymus arenarius*.

Tulipa sprengeri ▶
Height: 40cm/16in
Spread: 10cm/4in
Hardy, sun
The latest-flowering tulip, a pure red, with long, thin glossy green leaves. The slim bud is buff on the outside. A charming accompaniment to bearded iris, it also goes well with the lime-green of *Euphorbia* x *martinii* and *E. polychroma*. 'Red Shine' is a tall, late, soft red tulip, toning well with ornamental rhubarb, *Rheum palmatum* 'Atrosanguineum'.

Viburnum opulus 'Compactum'
Guelder rose
Height: 1.5m/5ft
Spread: 1.5m/5ft
Hardy, sun or light shade
Grow this for its fleshy, shiny red fruit, each about the size of a currant, hanging in clusters over a long period. In spring it has flat heads of white flowers. Plant with red-flowering cannas such as *Canna indica* 'Purpurea'.
▶

Vitis coignetiae
Crimson glory vine
Height: 15m/50ft
Spread: 6m/20ft
Hardy, sun or partial shade
A climber with huge leaves that turn rich red for a long period in the autumn, effective against a green background. Named clones are more reliably red. It needs space to be appreciated and is best grown up large trees or over structures such as pergolas.

Challenging ORANGE

With the vitality of glowing embers fanned by wind, orange is possibly the most exciting and challenging colour in the gardener's palette. Yet it is the one that many reject out of hand for any part of their garden.

◄ As orange as they come: the Mexican Tithonia rotundifolia (1.8m/6ft) is a coarse annual related to zinnia but its flowers are presented with the greatest style with the supporting stalk swelling just below (see the photograph of them in the Long Border on page 40, top left). The typical species is generally listed as 'Torch'; be sure this is what you buy and not 'Goldfinger', which is smaller, shorter-jointed, more congested and altogether meaner. Sow your seed in late spring and it will zoom away.

Strange, this. Oranges themselves, the fruit, are expected to be that bright colour (and how sumptuous they look when hanging on the tree surrounded by their own lush greenery). If not a sufficiently bright shade, they are dyed before reaching the market. Tomatoes are more muted, but still indisputably orange. You can grow yellow-fruited kinds, but they never give quite the same satisfaction and for culinary purposes, they seem anaemic. Who would buy a can of yellow tomatoes?

The real colour is typified by the naturally orange calendula, or pot marigold. When you have prepared a mixed green salad, scatter petals of this over it. Then, perhaps as an afterthought, scatter some blue flowers of borage, anchusa or chicory, to contrast with the orange. That looks good, you'll mutter, but then you should project and think how you might combine these colours with plants growing in the garden itself. Pot marigolds with blue love-in-a-mist, *Nigella damascena*, for instance, or with *Cynoglossum amabile*.

Of all colours, orange is the one that cries out the loudest for contrast. It is a waste to mingle it with red. Be bold and get it with purple, bay green, blue, even pink. I remember visiting a garden where there were neighbour plantings of the fiery, uncompromising orange *Lilium* 'Enchantment', with stiff heads of upright funnels, and of pink *Alstroemeria* Ligtu hybrids. The

▲ The pot marigold, Calendula officinalis, *is typically true orange – fully double in the best selected strains but, when it self-sows, reverting to the flower you see here. A hardy annual with a pleasing aroma, it contrasts nicely with the blue of* Cynoglossum amabile.

▼ *The Californian poppy,* Eschscholzia californica, *makes wonderful roadside drifts in its native land and is sometimes startlingly combined with bright pink clarkias. Look the other way? Certainly not. Try it out at home. Both are easy annuals.*

▶ *This rather amazing summer tapestry in Sarah Raven's Sussex garden has orange lilies as its centrepiece. Purple phlox, lime-green euphorbia and burnt orange* Helenium *'Moerheim Beauty' provide contrast. Sarah has written her own book,* The Bold & Brilliant Garden, *about this kind of gardening. She wanted to call it 'The Gaudy Garden', but it was thought that this title would not go down well in America.*

light on that July day was unyieldingly flat and shadowless. I was ready to be shocked. But they were beneath the dappled shade of trees which had an ideal calming influence, a mitigating factor that completely rescued the situation.

There is another type of alstroemeria, the old-fashioned Peruvian lily *A. aurea* (*A. aurantiaca*), which is itself yellowy-orange. It is a great colonizer and ideally sited in a drift beneath trees, livening up the woodland garden at a difficult time of year, in July, at Stourton House in Somerset. The clone called 'Dover Orange' is a richer shade and would look even better.

But to return to the possibilities of orange with pink: in August we have a nerve-testing contrast. There is the poker, *Kniphofia uvaria* 'Nobilis', 2.4m/8ft tall and purest orange. Its foliage is thoroughly untidy and needs to be hidden, which I do behind a great quilt of pink border phlox; not a harsh pink but bright, and in two shades. Don't ask me the name. One picks up phloxes from friends and names them after them or their homes. I call this one Doghouse Pink, because it came from Doghouse Farm, which was originally a pub, The Dog. So it goes.

Orange and pink; what next? Some of my friends looked and wondered. They could see that, although against the rules, it worked *in its setting*, and that's the point. Look at the photograph on pages 2-3 and you will see what I'm getting at. The border is backed by a dark green hedge. Then there is a grey-leaved, lavender-coloured buddleja, 'Lochinch', a large area of American Joe Pye weed, *Eupatorium purpureum* 'Atropurpureum' (1.8m/6ft) and cardoons, *Cynara cardunculus* (2.7m/9ft), with candelabrums of mauve thistle-heads. In front of these, the kniphofia; then the phlox, and that has a fringe of white Chinese chives, *Allium tuberosum*, as an apron before the stone-paved path. So it is a real community with a setting, not an indigestible dose of medicine taken without alleviating food.

Here is a June planting to make you blink. The daisy, *Anthemis sancti-johannis* (75cm/30in), is just about the purest shade of light orange that you could imagine, both in its disc and its rays. We planted a large patch of it next to the magenta-purple, dark-centred *Geranium psilostemon*. Mitigating neighbours at hand included the soft peachy 'Apricot' foxglove (*Digitalis purpurea*) and an airy blue larkspur, close to the wild type, of which a correspondent had sent me seed. The anthemis is short-lived and best treated as a biennial.

Bright colour is especially welcome in late winter and early

▲ Here is a spread of kniphofias, red-hot pokers, which are typically orange-hot, as are fire coals; not red. Seen here with Tithonia rotundifolia and, in the foreground, yellow Crocosmia 'Citronella'.

▶ The rather curiously shaped Kniphofia rooperi (1.2m/4ft) is late flowering. Seen here in mid-October with a background of the beautiful glaucous-leaved Melianthus major.

◀ Kniphofia uvaria 'Nobilis' in late summer against a column of Clematis 'Jackmanii Superba', trained up a pole. This is a giant among pokers. Some are quite tiny but are apt to get lost in a mixed border hurly-burly.

▶ The pokers of Kniphofia linearifolia (1.2m/4ft) all appear in a glad rush in October and look super against pampas grass, Cortaderia selloana 'Pumila' (top). The poker has bright green foliage, which is quite an asset in summer. Slightly taller at 1.5m/5ft, 'Lord Roberts' (bottom), named after a general of the Boer and First World Wars, is quite

an old cultivar, as its name suggests. Its pokers are slender and orange-red, with just a subtle hint of pink. Seen here with orach against the drying inflorescences of one of the best of all ornamental grasses, Calamagrostis x acutiflora 'Karl Foerster', which continues to be an asset till cut down in March.

▲ My favourite late-flowering tulip, 'Dillenburg', whose orange colouring is subtly flushed with pink on the outer petals. I grow it with a sort of wallflower, the mauve Erysimum linifolium, itself at its best in late spring and raised from seed sown the previous summer.

spring, when grey skies have made us feel starved of light and our own vitality is, perhaps, low. None better, then, than the February-flowering *Crocus flavus* subspecies *flavus* (*C. aureus*). Although its flowers are small, they are a far intenser orange than the familiar Dutch yellow crocus, and it self-sows, which is a great asset when a colony is just what you want. It will naturalize in a meadow setting and contrast well with another great, early-flowering and colonizing species, the mauve *C. tommasinianus*.

A little later in spring we have the glory of tulips. One of the earlier kinds is a *Tulipa fosteriana* hybrid called 'Orange Emperor'. The blooms are quite large, a soft orange and with a green stripe down the centre of each outer petal for quite a while before reaching full maturity. I rather enjoy a colour harmony, in this case, with the stiff spear leaves, veined orange-brown, of *Libertia peregrinans* in front and *Spiraea japonica* 'Gold Mound' (which you can prune for height) at hand. That is pale yellow on its young foliage. As a companion for the tulip in other circumstances, you could use the contrasting deep blue of grape hyacinths (*Muscari*).

Mid-season comes one of my favourites of the Lily-flowered tulips, 'Ballerina', soft yet bright and such a pretty shape. Then, in May, and just about one of the latest, 'Dillenburg', which is orange but with a subtle pink flush on its outer segments. We like to bed this out above a carpet of mauve *Erysimum linifolium* but we also thread it through and between clumps of border perennials like *Phlox paniculata* cultivars, which it greatly enlivens in what might otherwise be a dull period in a border's calendar.

Orange with a pink flush is found in many other tulips, such as the beautiful Parrot, 'Orange Favourite'. But also in the strain of *Euphorbia griffithii* called 'Dixter'. This is a hardy perennial with a running rootstock, which flowers in April-May. The stems and leaves are purplish red, the inflorescence reddish orange, tinged with pink. The other widely grown cultivar is 'Fireglow', whose flower heads are a brighter shade of orange, but the whole plant is much greener and lacks any purplish-pink cast. These spurges should be grown in full sun, for best colour. They look well, at their time of flowering, with a libertia – *L. formosa*, *L. grandiflora* or a *L. ixioides* hybrid – which has tufts of narrow, iris-like leaves and sprays of small white flowers.

We must not, as part of the spring scene, forget the bold and architectural crown imperial, *Fritillaria imperialis*; that is typically orange, slightly dusky. Really, I like to see it grouped near to its yellow-flowered version, which is similar in every way apart from

 ▲ The rather early-flowering Fosteriana hybrid tulip, 'Orange Emperor', harmonizes well in a border planting with Libertia peregrinans, whose stiff, iris-like evergreen leaves are a sort of burnt orange, brightest in winter and spring.

▶ The shapes of tulips are wonderfully varied. Those we call Lily-flowered are among the most graceful, here represented by 'Ballerina' (right), while 'Orange Favourite' (far right) is a typical Parrot, with rather ragged-edged petals and informally curved stems. The orange is flushed with pink and there is green in the developing flower, long retained.

43

▲ Euphorbia griffithii 'Dixter'. In this strain of a well-known hardy perennial spurge, the orange is intriguingly flushed with pink, while the leaves and stems are flushed purple. Full sun is required for best colour in its spring season. The plant makes colonies with its horizontally travelling rhizomes. They can be interplanted with small, early spring-flowering bulbs.

▶ Once again, orange is well partnered by its lime-green Euphorbia characias background in Beth Chatto's garden. The crown imperial, Fritillaria imperialis, is a magnificently structured plant, the bell flowers highlighted by the dark stems supporting them. The entire picture is built up by structural and colour contrasts.

colour. These bulbs, while growing, have a strong mixed odour of fox and garlic. I have never grown them well, but some gardeners have sheaves of them every year, apparently without effort. They increase well in Beth Chatto's stony soil, with yellow and lime-green euphorbias *E. characias* making a good background.

A May planting for the edge of a border that I enjoy, though the plants may get in the way of summer effects later, is of *Geum* 'Borisii' with a deep violet strain of *Viola cornuta*. The geum has single flowers on quite short stems (30cm/12in) and they are a clean shade of deep orange.

Hedychium, of the ginger family, are often on the tender side, though not as tender, in southern England, as many suppose. *H. densiflorum* (90cm/36in) is perfectly hardy and makes a dense colony with its superficial rhizomes. Its flowers, in August, are a biscuity colour, but far more impressive is Kingdon Ward's introduction, 'Assam Orange'. It makes dense spikes of intense orange flowers. They do not last for long, but there is a good succession. More thrilling still is *H. coccineum* in the clone 'Tara', which Tony Schilling introduced from Nepal. Its imposing canna-like leaves, in two ranks, are crowned by a quite broad, lively yet soft orange inflorescence.

Soft orange can be a charming colour and not in the least frightening. You find it in an old *Crocosmia* cultivar, 'Solfatare' (45cm/18in), which has coppery leaves and apricot-orange flowers. I like to see this pushing through the tangled grey foliage of *Artemisia alba* 'Canescens'. A number of poppy species have apricot-orange flowers, notable among them, in its own individual way, *Papaver spicatum*, which has intensely woolly, grey foliage. The flowers appear, in early summer, on a spike, opening along it over a period, in a seemingly haphazard way. The flowers are fragile, unfurling in the morning and shattering by noon – no use if you are a morning shopper or worker. An oriental poppy, unfortunately named 'Beauty Queen', is a favourite with me; apricot orange and bleaching attractively enough along its petal margins on the second day.

Then there is the bricky orange of *Glaucium flavum* f. *fulvum* (60cm/24in), with each flower lasting for a day. This is a horned poppy, the more normal colour yellow. Its crimped, pinnate foliage grows in loose rosettes and is intensely glaucous grey – really beautiful even in winter. It is a short-lived perennial but easily raised from seed. For spring effect, we interplant it with red species tulips.

In late summer and autumn, I can rely on *Zauschneria californica*, within which species I find 'Glasnevin' (23cm/9in) the most satisfying cultivar. It has a running rootstock and is excellent between the cracks in a retaining wall. I also grow 'Olbrich Silver', which has grey foliage, but it is comparatively shy-flowering. 'Glasnevin' bears a long succession of tubular flowers in a clean, pure shade of orange. Most cheering.

A large proportion of the orange-flowered plants that I must have are annuals or tender perennials. The best orange-flowered canna is the 2m/7ft *C.* 'Wyoming', its colour set off by bronze leaves. I have seen it looking very good in the evening, either side of a Cambridge college doorway with white *Nicotiana alata*, whose flowers only stiffen and expand towards sunset. But the canna also goes well with the tall white *Cosmos bipinnatus* 'Purity'. And I like to have that with the tremendously popular *Dahlia* 'David Howard' (1.8m/6ft). In fact the three together make an excellent trio. This dahlia is a neat, small decorative with apricot-orange flowers and darkish foliage. It flowers abundantly over a long season.

A tall annual that you can associate with these sorts of plants in a scheme of semi-tropical mood is the zinnia-like *Tithonia rotundifolia* 'Torch' (1.8m/6ft) (avoid the mini-version, 'Goldfinger', which is altogether mean). Its orange, Mexican-hat-style flowers are held proudly upright on a stalk which swells below the flower – a good design for a candlestick. To these four, for good measure, add some castor oil plants, *Ricinus communis*, whose lush, palmate foliage is rich reddish purple in the 1.8m/6ft strain, 'Carmencita'. It has prickly red seed heads, which makes for added interest.

There is a section of *Cosmos*, seed strains grouped under *C. sulphureus*, in which the flowers are in some shade of orange, usually quite deep and rich. When they are good, they are very very good, but English summers are not really hot enough for them and a heavy soil will make matters worse. Having started, perhaps, with a glorious burst of blossom in July, a heavy rain will start up botrytis and there'll be nothing further on offer.

This will be as good a place as any to introduce the little-encountered mask flower, *Alonsoa warscewiczii* (38cm/15in), which hails from Chile and is generally treated as an annual. The rotate flowers are presented upside-down, according to normal expectations. They are small, but numerous and borne along loose spikes, of a pure shade of orange, almost scarlet. I prefer the

▲ *Like many other cannas, C. 'Striata' holds its leaves upright, displaying their shape and receiving shadows from neighbouring plants. They are also translucent, so their colouring and veining can be admired, especially in low sunlight. The flowers of this and the pinky-red-variegated 'Durban' are orange.*

▶ *Orange theming with dahlia 'David Howard' and the finest of all orange cannas, 'Wyoming'. The bunches of silken flowers are greatly at the mercy of the weather and you need to remove (pull off) dead blooms frequently.*

▶▶ *A haze of colour in our Exotic Garden, early autumn. Dahlia 'David Howard', Cosmos bipinnatus 'Purity' and, in the background, a slightly tender shrub, Escallonia bifida. This has starry white flowers in late August and September, which are a magnet to butterflies, notably (but in different years) Tortoiseshells, Painted Ladies and Red Admirals. Deep mauve Verbena bonariensis is mixed in.*

▲ *Burnt orange Helenium 'Moerheim Beauty' contrasts with Salvia x superba. Their first flowering, seen here, is in early July, but both will flower freely a second time if dead-headed after the first crop.*

▼ *The poppy, Papaver 'Fireball', is quite short-stemmed and flowers in late spring. It is a ferocious runner, not to be let loose in polite society.*

slightly rangy habit of the type-plant to bushier, dwarfened strains, and I would always avoid the salmon-coloured strain, which entirely misses the point. It mixes well with the purple of *Browallia americana*, both plants being long-flowering and of roughly the same habit.

African marigolds (*Tagetes erecta*) can be splendid if the breeders have allowed them to make decent-sized, widely branching plants to two or three feet and have not absurdly dwarfened them so that you have large, blobby flowers on much too low a structure. My favourite strain has gone out of commerce (it would), so I hardly know what to recommend now but besides a big plant you want to look out for fully double blooms in a *deep* shade of orange – much more effective than the lighter orange kinds. Now bed them out with the bluey-mauve *Ageratum* 'Blue Horizon' seed strain (not many seeds in a packet, I warn you). This has a freely branching habit to 60cm/24in and both annuals flower on and on.

The brightest and most dominant orange ever seen in gardens is that of the Siberian wallflower, which is an *Erysimum* (*E. x allionii*) and may simply be listed as Siberian (45cm/18in). Of upright habit, it flowers a little later than the more normal bedding wallflowers and its sweet scent has a different quality. If you grow it near to paving, it will seed into the cracks. I like to use it in my mixed border, but not too much at a time and you can give a wide spacing to the plants, allowing other kinds to intervene, such as the pure white *Allium neapolitanum* (30cm/12in), which is at its best in late May. Most gardeners feel bound to say they hate the Siberian wallflower, but the truth is they are frightened of its uncompromising colour. I see no problem. No one is asking you to grow wadges of it, but it would be a shame to miss out altogether.

Almost as bright, but less aggressively presented, are the clean orange daisies of *Osteospermum hyoseroides*, a quickly growing annual which we often treat as a catch crop, since its season is relatively short. From a March sowing under glass, it will be flowering by the end of May and for the next month. Stop the seedlings once and never let them get crowded. A bushy plant is the aim. We actually go to the trouble of giving each plant a small stake and one tie. It gives you a buzz to see newly unfurled flowers each morning – they are such a bright and cheering colour. Soon after midday, they are tiring and their rays roll back upon themselves, to await the next morning. I like these with blue-flowered annuals.

▲ Pilosella aurantiaca *(better known as Hieracium aurantiacum) is a perennial meadow ingredient, especially prevalent in Scotland. It has a running rootstock and makes early summer-flowering colonies of great distinction, on account of its unusual burnt orange colouring, which is quite distinct from any other meadow plant.*

This leads us into a whole section of sun-sensitive, South African veldt daisies – gazania, osteospermum, arctotis (into which venidium has now been subsumed), ursinia. They are maddening and gladdening by turns, refusing to open wide unless conditions are just right, but giving you a great thrill when they are right. I travelled to Cape Province especially to see them, in August-early September, just as their spring is starting. They will fill a whole landscape where shrub scrub has been cleared and a crop has been taken on the shifting cultivations principle. These daisies are mainly white, pale yellow or orange, and it is the patches of orange that glow the most intensely. Sometimes the orange kinds were growing next to a small, magenta daisy, with a yellow eye, *Senecio elegans*. Would you have recoiled in horror, seeing that this was nature's own work? Of course not; it was a delight.

I saw many wild *Gladiolus* on that trip; dainty, fragile little things, far removed from the muscular monsters that are our florists' pride. And the most enchanting of these wildings was *G. alatus* (23cm/9in), with about five flowers to a stem, of a soft yet lively orange; the three, narrow, lowest petals, forming a bib, were green, with orange tips.

A rich tapestry of as many colours as possible is the ideal for a meadow flora, with green the overriding leitmotif. Orange, a kind of burnt orange, none too common in our palette, makes wonderful swathes of colour in many Scottish meadows and along

▲ Bomarea caldasii *is a perennial herbaceous twining climber, closely allied to* Alstroemeria. *Its clusters of orange flowers are very striking but too sparsely produced in the British climate, where its hardiness is only so-so. Late summer and autumn.*

their road verges, in June. This is the hawkweed, once *Hieracium*, now *Pilosella aurantiaca*. I am still trying to acclimatize it in East Sussex. It was originally introduced, but its stronghold in Britain is the north. In the south, the similarly coloured (but not nearly so widespread) *P. aurantiaca* subsp. *carpathicola* is the more likely meadow component. It has a running rootstock and would be hard to control if introduced to border life.

Of climbing plants with orange flowers, the most obvious example is the commonest form of nasturtium, *Tropaeolum majus*. It should never be underrated. A curtain of it clothing a north-facing fence is a memorable sight. It behaves as an annual in our climate but regenerates from self-sown seed. However, its performance is remarkably unpredictable. It hates drought, but under conditions too wet and well nourished, hides its beauty behind excess of foliage. It is also maddeningly subject to two pests: black aphids and the larvae of the Large White butterfly. If you spray against these, you are more than likely to upset the nasturtiums. If their enveloping growth is controlled, climbing nasturtiums can be a great asset in a border's interwoven tapestry. I like a big quilt of the mauve, spidery-flowered *Aster sedifolius*, in my August border. A few swags of nasturtiums filtering through this makes for a stunning contrast, but will the nasturtium oblige at the vital moment? Try and see!

The June-flowering honeysuckle, *Lonicera* x *tellmanniana*, can make dramatic impact up a not too domineering tree or against a shaded wall (shade suits the majority of climbing honeysuckles). It is not scented, but you can't have everything.

Bomarea is a genus I should dearly like to grow better, but it is on the borderlines of hardiness. *B. caldasii* is certainly worth a stab against a sheltered wall (it climbs over a *Cotoneaster horizontalis* for me). It is entirely herbaceous and an obvious relative of *Alstroemeria*. Each shoot terminates in a pendent cluster of narrowly funnelled flowers in gloriously warm shades of orange. They continue until the first frosts but are not as numerous as I should wish. In California, they make a far greater impression and a number of species are used. Probably we should experiment with more of them in England and Ireland.

Thunbergia alata has to be treated as an annual in Britain, which limits the amount of growth it can make to one season's. But it is a charming filler, to ramble over shrubs. The flowers are rotate, expanding from a tube, and are typically orange, which I like best, although you usually have to buy seed in a mixture,

which includes weaker shades. Always, there is a black eye, hence black-eyed-Susan, competing with rudbeckias given that name.

There are many orange fruits and seeds, often verging upon scarlet. One that is most obviously orange is *Iris foetidissima*, which is generally grown only for its seeds. They persist for a long while, the entire seed head lending itself to picking for indoor use. The plant is a somewhat mundane evergreen, but a garden has many places in which it can be welcomed, as at the foot of a hedge, and it has a propensity to self-sowing. Such plants find themselves the right sites for you, where you wouldn't (or couldn't) have planted anything else (as in a tight paving crack), and you are glad to let them get on with the good work.

You might like to grow a rose with orange hips alongside *Salvia involucrata* 'Bethellii' (1.2m/4ft), whose terminal inflorescences are in a shouting shade of rosy magenta. An artist friend gathered the two ingredients from my garden and painted them together, so as to show me that this team would work. She was right.

Wild arums (*Arum maculatum*) have clubs of orange berries, some 23cm/9in tall, while the rest of the plant is dormant. They can be a bit of a weed but most of us have a colony of the one known as *A. italicum* subsp. *italicum* 'Marmoratum', wherein the arrow leaves, between late autumn and late spring (unless killed off by heavy frost), have all their veins highlighted in very pale green, almost white (see page 98). But when a cohort of its fruit ripens, in August, there are no accompaniments, unless you create them. If your soil is not aggressively alkaline, try, behind the arums, *Kirengeshoma palmata* (60cm/24in), which, in late summer, has shuttlecock flowers in terminal clusters of pale yellow, to hover and bend over the orange fruit. Shade and a leafy soil suits these two.

Largest and most dramatic of orange fruits are those of turban gourds, and if you find you have bought seed of a good strain, save your own for other years and avoid more of the all-too-frequent disappointments from badly selected strains. Pick your gourds when they have started to colour and finish ripening them on a sunny windowsill.

So don't pretend that deep yellow or some sort of salmon is orange. Rise to the challenge and go for the real thing.

▲ The long hips of Rosa setipoda *always attract attention. Its single pink flowers are modestly charming. Setipoda means bristly-fruited. Well named.*

▼ The fruits of Arum italicum *and of our own native* A. maculatum *ripen in late summer when there is no foliage. I have seen them well contrasted with the soft yellow shuttlecock flowers of Kirengeshoma palmata drooping over them from behind.*

Alonsoa warscewiczii
Mask flower
Height: 38cm /15in
Spread: 35cm/14in
Tender, full sun
A perennial usually treated as an annual and grown from seed in the spring. Cuttings can also be overwintered inside. Choose the stronger orange to scarlet varieties. Its bright flowers, deep green leaves and red stems associate well with purple-flowered *Browallia americana*.

Alstroemeria aurea
Peruvian lily
Height: 90cm /36in
Spread: 45cm/18in
Hardy, full sun/light shade
An easy alstroemeria that spreads to form a colony or drift. The flowers are yellow or orange with streaks of dark red. 'Dover Orange' is a deeper orange, effective planted in drifts among spring-flowering azaleas or under trees as long as the shade is not too deep.

Anthemis sancti-johannis
Height: 75cm/30in
Spread: 60cm/24in
Hardy, full sun
A pure orange daisy for early to mid summer. It is perennial but only a short-lived one and will need replacing every year or every other year, although it will often self-sow by itself. For dramatic effect, plant it next to the magenta *Geranium psilostemon* or the purple spikes of *Salvia nemerosa* 'Ostfreisland'.

Calendula officinalis
Pot marigold
Height: 30-60cm/ 12-24in
Spread: 30-45cm/12-18in
Full sun/light shade
A hardy annual for any well-drained soil, with bright orange, daisy-like flowers, which are available either as singles or doubles. The plants are often lax and will sprawl a little. The seed can be sown where the plant is to flower in autumn or spring or under glass in spring. Plant with blue *Nigella damascena* or dazzling *Cynoglossum amabile*.

▲ Canna 'Wyoming'
Indian shot plant
Height: 2m/7ft
Spread: 60cm/24in
Tender, full sun
The best orange-flowered canna, with purple-bronze, large paddle-shaped foliage. Goes well with white-flowered plants such as *Nicotiana alata* or *Cosmos bipinnatus* 'Purity', also with the orange *Dahlia* 'David Howard'.

Crocus flavus subsp. *flavus*
Height: 8cm /3in
Spread: 5cm/2in
Hardy, full sun
Small typical crocus goblets of bright orange that brighten the late winter and early spring. Good for naturalizing as it will self-sow. Grow with contrasting mauve and purple *C. tommasinianus*.

▲ Dahlia 'David Howard'
Height: 1.8m/6ft
Spread: 45cm/18in
Tender, full sun
A Miniature Decorative dahlia with apricot-orange flowers that are darker in the centre, set off by foliage with a blackish tinge. It goes well with *Canna* 'Wyoming' or contrasting *Verbena bonariensis*.

Erysimum x *allionii*
Siberian wallflower
Height: 45cm/18in
Spread: 30cm/12in
Hardy, full sun
A short-lived perennial for any well-drained soil, usually treated as a biennial and grown from seed each year. The bright, rich orange flowers are sweetly scented.

Crocosmia x crocosmiiflora 'Solfatare'
Montbretia
Height: 45cm/18in
Spread: 15cm/6in
Hardy, full sun/light shade
Soft orange flowers from midsummer onwards, well set off by the bronze-tinged, strap-like leaves. The corms (bulbs) need to be divided when they become congested. It looks good growing through the grey foliage of *Artemisia alba* 'Canescens' and harmonizes well with *Zinnia* 'Chippendale'.

Euphorbia griffithii 'Fireglow'
Spurge
Height: 60cm/24in at flowering; 90cm/36in later
Spread: 50cm/20in
Hardy, full sun
Bright orange-red with green leaves; *E.g.* 'Dixter' is deeper orange-red with stems, leaves and leaf veins suffused with purple and red. The widely spaced rhizomes can be inter-planted with small early-flowering bulbs or winter-flowering crocuses. ▶

Fritillaria imperialis
Crown imperial
Height: 90cm/36in
Spread: 30cm/12in
Hardy, full sun
A bulbous perennial for late spring or early summer, with a cluster of orange bells hanging from a tall stem below a tuft of green leaves. The yellow form mixes well with the orange.

Geum 'Borisii'
Height: 30cm/12in
Spread: 30cm/12in
Hardy, full sun
An airy but compact plant for the edge of a summer border, with deep orange flowers held above the slightly hairy leaves. It associates well with deep blue flowers, such as the violet strains of *Viola cornuta* or *Veronica austriaca* subsp. *teucrium* 'Crater Lake Blue'.

Glaucium flavum
Yellow horned poppy
Height: 60cm /24in
Spread: 45cm/18in
Hardy, full sun
A stronger colour than the yellow-flowered species, *G.f.* forma *fulvum* has reddish-orange poppy-like flowers in summer. Its foliage is appealing glaucous grey and it has attractive, long seed pods. It is suitable for mixed borders. Although a perennial, it is short-lived and needs to be renewed from seed. Grow with red species tulips or *Eryngium* x *oliverianum*.

**Hedychium coccineum ▶
'Tara'**
Ginger lily
Height: 107cm /42in
Spread: 90cm/36in
Tender, sun or light shade
A showy plant with
conspicuous spikes of soft
orange flowers in late
summer and autumn. It
goes well with some of the
bright red dahlias, or, as a
contrast, the deep mauve
Verbena bonariensis.
Mulch well for the
winter or lift and store.
In *H. densiflorum* 'Assam
Orange' the flowers are a
more intense orange.

Kniphofia uvaria 'Nobilis'
Red hot poker
Height: 2.4m/8ft
Spread: 60cm/24in
Hardy, full sun
An evergreen plant with a
fountain of untidy, strap-like
leaves from which emerges
tall stems with tight heads
of orange flowers from late
summer onwards. For
contrast, plant with pink-
flowering phloxes or purple-
leaved, pink-flowered
Eupatorium purpureum
'Atropurpureum' or in front
of *Buddleja* 'Lochinch' and
next to *Artemisia lactiflora*.

▲ Lilium pomponium
Height: 90cm/3ft
Hardy, full sun
You may find this brilliant
turkscap lily when on
holiday in the south of
France. Resist the
temptation to take a bulb
home with you, if for no
better reason than it won't
stay with you for very long.

Osteospermum hyoseroides
Height: 45cm/18in
Spread: 25cm /10in
Tender, full sun
An annual with bright
orange daisies that are
only fully open during the
morning. They flower in
the early summer from a
March sowing. The foliage
is sticky and aromatic.
They go well with blue
annuals such as *Asperula
orientalis, Heliophila,
Felicia* or *Brachyscome*. ▼

**Tithonia rotundifolia
'Torch'**
Mexican sunflower
Height: 1.8m/6ft
Spread: 38cm/15in
Tender, full sun
An annual for high
summer with amazingly
pure, deep orange zinnia-
like flowers sitting on top
of thickened stems that
swell just below the flower.
Large, hairy heart-shaped
leaves will obscure the
stout canes needed to
support the long stems.
Associates well with
contrasting deep mauve
Verbena bonariensis,
especially when planted
amongst them.

Tropaeolum majus
Nasturtium
Height: 3m/10ft
Spread: 5m/16ft
Tender, full sun/light shade
An annual climbing plant
for non-alkaline soils, with
varying shades of trumpet-
shaped orange flowers
from summer onwards.

Tulipa 'Prinses Irene'
Height: 35cm/14in
Spread: 10cm/4in
Hardy, full sun
A dusky orange single mid-
season tulip. Another is
Lily-flowered 'Ballerina', a
mixture of yellow, orange
and red, with petals that
sweep up into a narrow
point. The Parrot 'Orange
Favourite' is orange
marked with green.
'Dillenburg' – orange with
a pink flush – comes later.
Plant amongst summer-
and autumn-flowering
perennials.
◀

True BLUES are Few

Blue flowers are in such demand, are such certain sellers, that nurserymen have to stretch the interpretation of the word to snapping point.

◀ *The 'Miss Jekyll' strain of love-in-a-mist,* Nigella damascena, *should be true blue, but you can never be sure of what will happen to a plant which can only be propagated from seed. It is a hardy, self-sowing annual but the best plants are obtained by controlled sowings under glass in autumn, the seedlings being potted individually and planted out in spring.*

More than half the flowers described as blue in seed lists and plant catalogues are some shade of mauve or purple. True-blue flowers are few.

Everybody loves blue. Blue eyes (in Nordic and Anglo-Saxon countries), candour ('he looked at me with those piercing blue eyes of his', could hardly be changed to brown eyes or green), innocence (anyone with blue eyes learns to use them to their own advantage).

Many gardeners insist on having a blue border. Gertrude Jekyll was a wise old bird. In *Colour in the Flower Garden*, she wrote: 'It is a curious thing that people will sometimes spoil some garden project for the sake of a word. For instance, a blue garden, for beauty's sake, may be hungering for a group of white Lilies, or for something of palest lemon-yellow, but it is not allowed to have it because it is called the blue garden. . . . Surely the business of the blue garden is to be beautiful as well as to be blue. My own idea is that it should be beautiful first, and then just as blue as may be consistent with its best possible beauty. Moreover, any experienced colourist knows that the blues will be more telling – more purely blue – by the juxtaposition of rightly placed complementary colour.'

More than any other colour, blue needs contrast near to it, to prevent its looking dull. (Some blue flowers are irremediably dull

▲ The deep, almost sulky blue of Aconitum 'Spark's Variety' needs highlighting; here by yellow-leaved catalpa and ivy.

▶▲ Examples of highlighting blue with another colour. The Spanish bluebell, Hyacinthoides hispanica 'Chevithorn' (above, centre), is backed by the young foliage of Fuchsia magellanica var. gracilis 'Aurea'. This large clump-forming bluebell has the great advantage, when used in borders, of not self-sowing. Columns of elegant, willowy leaves on Helianthus salicifolius (far right) make a foreground for spires of blue delphiniums.

▶ Salvia patens is normally Oxford blue. The 'Cambridge Blue' variant is light in colour and just as desirable in its way. Asclepias tuberosa (60cm/24in), with rich orange flowers borne in umbels, makes a splendid contrast, if summers are hot enough to please it.

in a lifeless sort of way.) Most gardeners cheat by including mauve – especially lavender and campanula-blue (which is never pure) – in their blue border. Miss Jekyll kept these colours separate at either end of her famous colour-themed border, and she was right. They do not help each other, being close in colour, yet the off-blues muddy by comparison.

Let's start with two stars in the blue firmament – delphiniums and salvias. Delphiniums are the most obviously blue flowers, though they include many other delightful shades and these should not be despised. In large flower arrangements, the ideal contrast in colour and form is achieved with spikes of blue delphiniums and double pink peonies, like 'Sarah Bernhardt'. On the other hand, the contrast of a deep, cobalt blue delphinium with the flat-topped corymbs of bright, mustard-yellow *Achillea filipendulina*, is too crude. In preference, site a blue delphinium near to the pale, greeny-yellow tree scabious, *Cephalaria alpina*, which grows to nearly 1.8m/6ft.

If you find the traditional delphinium rather too stiff and self-assertive, remember the lower-growing Belladonna types, whose main spike is scarcely more dominant than the side branches. They are good blenders, for instance with pink sidalceas, or with the pale yellow fluffs of *Thalictrum flavum* subsp. *glaucum*, whose blue leaves are especially appropriate.

Salvias include most colours and there are pure blues among them. Some of the best are none too hardy but their management is not difficult, once the problem is recognized. *Salvia uliginosa* (1.8m/6ft) is invaluable in the late summer and autumn border. It is a colonizer, straying from its centre, and carries short spikes of light blue flowers, each with a white fleck at its centre. Wasted on its own, this contrasts splendidly with the more solid form of Small Decorative, Cactus, Single or Collerette dahlias, perhaps in yellow or pink, although red would be good, too. If the dahlias are too close to the questing salvia, they will be in danger of being swamped. Although we leave this salvia in the border, we also lift and pot up pieces in the autumn, to overwinter in absolute safety under glass. Come spring the border group will need re-organizing, planting up gaps in its centre and bringing the strayed bits back to where they are needed.

Another favourite is *Salvia guaranitica* (1.8m/6ft) and its closely related hybrids. Best by far is 'Blue Enigma', which is rich, deep (but not too deep) blue and it has lustrous, dark green foliage. This has large tuberous roots, again of borderline hardiness, so we cover stock left outside with protective litter, but also overwinter young plants under glass. These are raised from soft cuttings taken in April or May as the young shoots come up from an old stool. Old plants will start flowering in late June and may run out of steam in the autumn. However, spring-struck cuttings will be fresh and looking their best in October and will team up well with dahlias, also from late-struck cuttings. We recently used the pure red, Small Semi-cactus 'Alva's Doris' and both flowered with panache at 90cm/36in or so. Deep blue contrasts nicely with orange and red.

The Oxford blue *Salvia patens* (45cm/18in) is an old favourite, often used in bedding. This species has quite large flowers, but seldom more than two at a time on each spike, so it is inclined to look threadbare, especially later in the season. Cutting your plants over, mid-season, helps to give them a new lease of energy. Again tuberous-rooted and of untrustworthy hardiness. You can overwinter old tubers in damp soil, taking cuttings from the young shoots in spring, if you want to, or you can raise it quickly from seed to flower, sowing in March or April, and saving your own seed from year to year. The light blue 'Cambridge Blue' is as good in its way, although not a free producer of seed.

There are not many blue-flowered shrubs, so they are correspondingly precious. *Caryopteris* x *clandonensis* (90cm/36in)

in one of its deeper blue cultivars, passes muster. They flower along the nodes of their young shoots in late summer. 'Worcester Gold' has yellowish leaves in contrast to its blue flowers, but already doing their bit before flowering starts. Sometimes I find it anaemic, at others, rather effective. Try and see. It will probably need the company of something solid to justify its own flimsiness and *Sedum* 'Herbstfreude' (Autumn Joy) will fulfil this. That changes gradually from green, through dusky pink to deep, dusky red.

Like caryopteris, *Perovskia atriplicifolia* (1.2m/4ft), the Russian sage, prefers light soil and an open, sunny site. From midsummer, it makes panicles of small blue flowers offset by greyish stems and leaves. Give it a hard cut-back each spring.

The tender plumbago, *P. auriculata* (better known as *P. capensis*), an immensely vigorous scrambler with light blue flowers, needs glass in our climate, though some public gardens bed it out as a dot plant for the summer. This seldom works well. However, its considerably hardier relation, *Ceratostigma willmottianum*, can be a great success as a garden permanency, particularly if it can bring its old wood through the winter alive, so as to make a bigger bush (for its habit is bushy) and to start flowering far earlier, at midsummer, rather than in early autumn, if winter killed its old growth back to the ground. So, a reasonably sheltered and sunny position for this fine shrub. It may grow 1m/3ft tall in the open and more against a warm wall. At Beth Chatto's, it looks beautiful in front of the vigorous, shrubby *Artemisia arborescens*, which is grown entirely for its grey foliage and is happiest on very light soil, but none too hardy even then. I like the ceratostigma in a variety of mixed border situations – with red-and-purple fuchsias, for instance, if the soil is damp enough. Its dead-heads are charming through the winter and it shouldn't be pruned or tidied at all until late spring, then only removing dead wood or died-back shoot tips.

On acid soils, hydrangeas can be true blue, as against purple or mauve if the soil is not quite acid enough, and pink or red if it is neutral or alkaline. Blue suits some hydrangeas better than others. Among the best is *Hydrangea serrata* 'Bluebird' (1.2m/4ft), which blues readily given the faintest hint of acidity in the soil. A Lacecap, it is one of the hardiest. The Hortensia, *H. macrophylla* 'Générale Vicomtesse de Vibraye' (1m/40in or more) has buns of small flowers which are an undistinguished pale pink on alkaline soil, but change to a charming light, sky blue, when acid. This is an excellent tub plant and its colouring can there be regulated,

▲ *The blue, late-summer flowers of* Caryopteris x clandonensis *are provided with their own highlighting – lime-green foliage in the cultivar 'Worcester Gold'. On their own, the leaves make quite a contribution earlier in the season.*

▼ *Hydrangea* macrophylla *'Générale Vicomtesse de Vibraye' has large bun heads of small flowers. Hydrangeas like abundant moisture in the growing season.*

▲ The evergreen species of Ceanothus, *which are native to the Pacific Ocean littoral of North America, are rarely as blue in the wild as the selected forms are in British gardens. 'Puget Blue' is one of the bluest currently available. Striking and unusual in its late spring-flowering season. Ceanothus are fast-growing shrubs but not very long-lived and damaged in hard winters.*

first by the compost that you start with and second, if necessary, by waterings with aluminium sulphate to acidify the soil.

A red brick wall suits blue ceanothus as a background. The deciduous ceanothus are in weak shades of off-blue and, although conveniently summer-flowering and hardy, need not detain us. I am thinking of the evergreen kinds, most of which flower in spring or early summer and may not be altogether hardy. But they have an amazing abundance of blossom and are exceedingly striking. There's nothing else we grow to touch them. All are fast-growing but outstandingly so is the early-flowering *Ceanothus arboreus* 'Trewithen Blue' (6m/20ft if it survives wind damage). It is often out in March. This is a show-stopper, but so liable to break up or to succumb to frost, that you'll be doing well to keep it in good order for four years. As soon as it starts to worry you, get rid of it. A proper recovery is almost unheard of. An early-flowering crimson red rhododendron would make a good companion, especially in the climate of Cornwall, where summers can be guaranteed cool. *Rhododendron strigillosum* is unusually early.

▲ *Agapanthus flower mid- to late summer, but they do not flower well if hemmed in by other plants, so combinations are not always easy to arrange. The obvious one for contrast with blue forms would seem to be orange crocosmias, seen in the background here.*

▼ *Echinops, the globe thistles, have intriguing flower heads but are generally pretty coarse plants with a shortish summer flowering season. E. ritro subsp. ruthenicus, here.*

R. neriiflorum, with neater foliage and slightly later, but still early, might be even better, and no matter if it were somewhat lower growing.

Agapanthus are mostly in some shade of blue, which is what makes them so popular, although the white kinds are also attractive. The larger the flower umbel and the larger the flowers, the more tender the plant is likely to be. So it is with the kinds that are most often grown for display in tubs, but are moved under cover for the winter. However, a great many agapanthus are virtually hardy in Britain. Gardeners get over-excited by them and plant them in rows, with no supporting cast, which is dull in the extreme. Try them with red or orange kniphofias, for instance, having the same August season. I am growing a September-flowering, deep blue variety, 'Loch Hope' with a fairly late, orange crocosmia. The strap leaves of agapanthus are uninteresting. If grown where they are not too apparent, it helps.

The globe thistles of the genus *Echinops* (generally 1.2m/4ft) have globes of blue flowers but their midsummer season is too short and the plants, with their dark leaves, are unacceptably coarse. *E. bannaticus* 'Taplow Blue' is one of the best in this section. Don't associate it with other blues, for heaven's sake, but liven it up with bright neighbours like phloxes. *E. ritro* subsp. *ruthenicus* (only 60cm/24in), grown from seed, looked scintillating on Thompson & Morgan's trial ground, but seems short-lived on our heavy clay. We are still fighting for it. Some day, I have hopes of finding the echinops for me.

Of greater interest are the eryngiums, known as sea hollies.
The bluest that I have met is *Eryngium* x *oliverianum* (90cm/36in),
which we have had in the same spot in our garden since as far
back as I can remember. It has thick tap roots and does not take
kindly to disturbance, but is, none the less, propagated from root
cuttings. Flowering in July, there is a muted blue cone of tiny
flowers surrounded by an imposing ruff of spiny bracts, the whole
subtended by stems of an astonishing metallic blue – that is, if
you grow it in full sun, which is essential. This is undoubtedly a
plant that needs strong colours near to it, the orange of crocosmias,
the yellow of coreopsis. In its turn, it will tone these colours down.
On its own, even this eryngium is a dull dog. The slightly earlier-
flowering *E. alpinum* is in the same style but its ruff of bracts is
denser and deeper and they are soft to the touch.

Several blue eryngium species have small inflorescences but a
lot of them. This creates a soft blue haze. *E.* x *tripartitum*
(60cm/24in) is one such. I just wish that they – all of them –
didn't flop about so much. They need discreet support but
combining discretion with efficiency is not entirely simple.

Baptisia australis (90cm/36in) is like a lupin with a pedigree,
with clean lines and an elegant habit. The deep blue flowers, in
June, are well spaced along the spikes and there is plenty of
supporting, light green foliage. This, indeed, makes the best
contrast to the flowers. Baptisia is in less need of companion
planting than most blue flowers.

Many veronicas are early-flowering perennials and, as garden

plants, their dullness after flowering militates against them. The May-flowering species that we knew as *Veronica teucrium* should be *V. austriaca* subsp. *teucrium*. 'Crater Lake Blue' (45cm/18in) is typical of the best, with a dense array of deep, pure blue spikes. It generally needs support. Looks good with orange or red geums. 'Shirley Blue' (23cm/9in) makes more of a loose mat for the margin of a border where there is a hard edge it can flop over. Again, a short season, as has *V. peduncularis* 'Georgia Blue' (15cm/6in), which is quite a deep shade. In its April season, it contrasts well with the little Triandrus *Narcissus* 'Hawera', which is quite a miniature with heads of cool yellow, nodding flowers. *V. gentianoides* (30cm/12in) makes basal rosettes of rather gentian-like leaves, and the flower spikes in May are a cool shade of light blue. I am fond of this plant but still find it hard to place. It has a prettily variegated-leaved form, 'Variegata', which also flowers freely, though less robustly.

Anchusa azurea* (syn. *A. italica*) (1.8m/6ft) is blue when at its best but all too inclined to be adulterated with purple. 'Opal' is a cultivar to look out for, though not always true to name. I hope the breeders will give their renewed attention to this flower. Although perennial, I find it best treated as a biennial, renewing your own stock from root cuttings, which can be taken at planting-out time in the autumn. It flowers in early summer and mixes well with a white strain of sweet rocket, *Hesperis matronalis*, which can also be bedded out and treated as a biennial. With anything of as bright a colour as orange, crimson and scarlet oriental poppies, the duller-toned anchusas will sink into nonentity.

What of the famous blue poppies, of the genus *Meconopsis*? They caused a greater stir, through the twentieth century, than any other blue flower. Yet, in southeast England, I do not grow them at all. They are hardy, but detest summer heat. The cool air of the north is what suits them and I am happy to meet them in Scotland, in early summer. *M. betonicifolia* and the more perennially inclined *M. grandis* (both 1m/40in) are the two principal species, although cultivars of the cross between these two, *M. x sheldonii*, generally produce the most satisfactory results. For contrast nothing could suit them better than their own cushion of yellow stamens.

The most exciting gentians, like *Gentiana verna*, need the alpine enthusiast's specialist care. I would rather see them at home in their alpine meadows and keep that memory with me. *G. acaulis*, with blue trumpets on a mat-forming plant, is easy

◀ Baptisia australis, from the USA, is a deep-rooted perennial resembling a refined lupin, with widely spaced flowers. Its own fresh green foliage makes as good a colour contrast as any. Flowers early summer. Seed is the obvious method of increase.

▶ Meconopsis grandis with a background of foxgloves. To be so luxuriant, this has to be in Scotland, but open woodland conditions with acid leaf soil and abundant moisture are the necessaries for success without undue further effort. This species is more reliably perennial than many, but still needs dividing and replanting every three years or so.

◀ A typical early-summer-flowering Anchusa azurea, 'Dropmore' being a selected clone though unlikely to be true to name. Plants are best discarded the second summer. Follow on with a late-sown annual like Cosmos bipinnatus 'Purity'.

▶ Meconopsis x sheldonii, the cross between M. betonicifolia and M. grandis, has given rise to the most satisfactory blue poppies in cultivation, many of them being named clones. In southeast England, they tend to die after flowering and seeding, but in a cool, damp climate, special conditions will not need to be provided, so long as they have good leaf soil in which to grow and they are divided and replanted every few years.

▲ The blue pimpernel, Anagallis monellii *subsp.* linifolia, *is grown as an annual. It has a low, scrambling habit and its flower colouring is so intense that it is often mistaken for a gentian. It has a long season, the flowers opening in sunshine. They are highlighted here with a dwarf yellow marigold.*

▶▲ *The willow gentian,* Gentiana asclepiadea, *is a deep-rooted woodland perennial flowering late in summer. If possible, it should never be moved. Here grown in front of the bramble,* Rubus cockburnianus *'Goldenvale', which has bright greeny yellow foliage. But this is apt to swamp its neighbours and must be controlled during its growing season. The gentian also looks well with the pale yellow shuttlecock flowers of* Kirengeshoma palmata. *The gentian often self-sows.*

▶ *One of the many hybrids of early summer-flowering* Iris sibirica, *'Placid Waters', beautifully highlighted by Bowles' golden sedge,* Carex elata *'Aurea', at Glen Chantry in Essex. Both plants are moisture lovers and can be grown in boggy ground that is under water from time to time. None of these irises are true blue, it must be admitted.*

enough to grow, although it does not flower freely in every garden. Its dense mats need dividing every third year if they are not to go blind. I combined this once with quilled red pomponette daisies (*Bellis perennis*) behind, and that was nice. The easiest-going gentian for garden use (although it sometimes refuses to flourish where you plant it, yet self-sows where you'd have thought it would be unhappy), is the woodland species *G. asclepiadea* (60cm/24in, arching), called willow gentian. It flowers in August and needs neutral or acid soil. Its blue trumpets line either side of a long, arching stem. It needs enlivening. If you can control it, the yellow-leaved bramble, *Rubus cockburnianus* 'Goldenvale', is in excellent contrast, but its spreading habits need checking annually. Often mistaken for a gentian, there's the annual blue-flowered pimpernel, *Anagallis monellii* subsp. *linifolia*.

Blue-flowered aquatics are rare but pickerel weed, *Pontederia cordata* (60cm/24in) is that. It grows in shallow water, as it might be near to a pondside bank, and flowers in August. This makes a smart-looking colony, with blunt-arrow leaves and dense spikes of small blue flowers. If you grow the old, easily naturalized *Crocosmia pottsii* (60cm/24in) so that it projects over the water from a neighbouring bank, its red colouring makes an assured contrast.

The first of the blue-flowered annuals that will come to mind is the cornflower, *Centaurea cyanus* (90cm/36in) and it will

▲ An old herbaceous favourite, the perennial cornflower, Centaurea montana, *makes a nice foreground for the white* Libertia ixioides *hybrid in early summer. If cut back after its first flush, the centaurea will flower again.*

▶ *Annual cornflowers,* Centaurea cyanus, *are included in the spectacular cornfield seed mix used on a field scale at The Old Vicarage, East Ruston, near to the east Norfolk coast. A completely open site is essential.*

▼ *My preferred strain of annual cornflower,* Centaurea cyanus *'Blue Diadem'.*

feature prominently in any cornfield seed mixture, blending happily with the widest range of colours. Another shorter weed of cultivation, which I saw in Syria, is the light blue *Asperula orientalis* (38cm/15in). It belongs to the bedstraw family, and bears heads of small, cruciform flowers in early summer, if sown in spring. Its flowering is ephemeral but I love to give it a run, from time to time, generally mixing it with orange flowers – calendulas and *Osteospermum hyoseroides.*

The self-sowing, hardy love-in-a-mist, *Nigella damascena* (38cm/15in), is blue in the well known 'Miss Jekyll' strain, which I consider the most typical. Best plants are obtained not from self-sowns left *in situ*, which are apt to starve each other out, but by potting autumn-germinated self-sowns individually in the autumn and planting them out in early spring. We thread them through our mixed borders.

The borage family is rich in blues, though many of them include a mauve element – bedding myosotis (forget-me-nots), for instance. Still, they make a blue impression and form a running theme through our borders in April and May. They are traditional carpeters for tulips, especially effective with pink tulips, as it might be the Lily-flowered 'China Pink'. Borage itself, *Borago*

▲ Forget-me-nots are the ideal carpet for tulips of any colour. We use self-sowing stock from year to year but a better quality is obtained by controlled sowings of selected seed strains. These will be of a more intense colouring and generally give rise to quite dumpy (I mean dwarf and compact) plants.

▼ In the Red chapter, we have seen this blue lyme grass, Leymus arenarius, contrasted with Salvia coccinea 'Lady in Red'. That can well be a follow-on to the colour theming shown here with Cynoglossum amabile, which can be grown as an annual or biennial, but is not entirely hardy.

officinalis, is blue-flowered but scarcely showy. More so is *Cynoglossum amabile* (60cm/24in), in one of its seed strains – a piercing light blue. It can be treated as annual or biennial but is not reliably winter-hardy. We plant it around our blue lyme grass, *Leymus arenarius*, which is a wickedly spreading perennial and needs calling to heel every year, but its young foliage is intensely blue. So there's an example of blue with blue, the contrast coming from flowers with leaves and from entirely different habits.

Omphalodes cappadocica (23cm/9in) is perennial and like a forget-me-not but more solid and purposeful. Get a deep blue cultivar like 'Cherry Ingram'. This is excellent in shade and I best enjoy it beneath the branches of a double red camellia, whose petals fall while still retaining their colour, and make pools around the blue omphalodes clumps. 'Starry Eyes' is an *O. cappadocica* cultivar with a palest blue rim around each deeper blue petal. It is winsome.

The climbing annual *Ipomoea tricolor* 'Heavenly Blue' is in a class of its own. If happy, it will, even in our climate, display itself thrillingly up a 1.8m/6ft wigwam of brushwood. The large trumpet flowers last only for a half-day, and make a dazzling show each fine August and September morning. Then they fade, to a rather nasty mauve and that's it till the next morning. You can also grow them up the netting that surrounds a tennis court. Or over any other support where they are not crowded out. We pop them in all over the place to give us surprises. You can keep them throughout in pots to climb in front of a verandah. You'll never, in

▲ If you have a red camellia that sheds its petals (rather than holding on to them till brown), as is the case with this old Camellia japonica *cultivar* called 'Margherita Coleoni', the carpet makes an admirable foil to the shade-tolerant blue Omphalodes cappadocica 'Cherry Ingram'.

▼ *Spring-flowering scillas, chionodoxas and the hybrid between them,* x Chionoscilla, *can be scattered through a whole lot of spring plantings, sometimes lifting them after flowering and replanting in autumn; sometimes leaving them indefinitely* in situ.

our climate, see too many of them as they are quite tricky to grow well. The seedlings hate to be cold, turning yellow and pinched. Hasten slowly is the motto. Don't sow till well into May and then under glass and in most areas it'll be best not to get them outdoors till late June.

Blue bulbs for spring include grape hyacinths, *Muscari*, which are obliging and have quite an extended spring season. It is a pity that the foliage of the easiest of them, *M. armeniacum* (38cm/15in), is so long and lanky. The double strain 'Blue Spike' (illustrated on page 168), when well grown from large bulbs, makes a great show. I like these with the deep butter yellow of jonquils (*Narcissus jonquilla*). *Chionodoxa*, albeit only a few inches high, are extremely willing; *C. luciliae* has a white centre; it can self-sow, in cultivated ground, say among deciduous shrubs, but an association for it might not be easily organized. The bigeneric hybrid x *Chionoscilla allenii*, with tufts of starry blue flowers, March-April, is a real goer. I like it with the young, greeny-yellow leaves of *Valeriana phu* 'Aurea'. *Scilla siberica* (10cm/4in) is quite a piercing shade of true blue. It will increase rapidly under border conditions but, with me, peters out if planted in my meadows. Some gardeners manage this successfully, perhaps on thinner turf.

All sorts of foliage plants are glaucous, which simply means greyish blue. Some hostas are notable, for instance *H*. 'Halcyon' whose neat, pointed leaves overlap like tiles on a roof. 'Buckshaw Blue' is a broad-leaved one that I used to go for and it was

striking, when young in front of the purplish foliage of *Rodgersia pinnata* 'Superba'. But whereas the rodgersia seems impervious to the attentions of slugs and snails, the hosta was an increasing reproach to me for doing nothing to control them. Reproachful plants are insupportable. Also, its leaves tarnish at the height of summer, so it went.

In quite a different vein, I've already mentioned the juvenile leaves of some eucalyptus making satisfying contrast to purple-leaved cannas. Another entirely different glaucous plant that I dote on is *Senecio serpens*. Of creeping, mat-forming habit, this is a succulent member of its tribe, with cylindrical leaves tapering to fine points. It can be bedded out for the summer and will spill over a hard border margin, but will not look right with soft-leaved plants. Rather I would suggest *Cotyledon orbiculata*, which has large, succulent grey leaves in prostrate rosettes. That, again, is tender but a good bedder. Perhaps you have a sunny ledge for these sorts of plants.

It is quite exciting when berries so far diverge from the scarlet colouring expected of them as to be blue – even bright blue. A bright blue berry, and shiny like porcelain, is that of *Clerodendrum trichotomum*. They are borne on a shapeless shrub (which, however, can be hard-pruned in spring) in loose panicles and are the more effective for each berry being framed by the fleshy pink lobes of the persistent calyx. At a stroke, you are presented with a fine colour contrast. This shrub needs all the heat it can get, if it is to fruit well.

Viburnum davidii, on female plants (some nurseries sell them sexed) has umbels of small blue berries, sometimes rather buried among its evergreen leaves. Not a bright blue and it is the same with *V. tinus*, laurustinus. You need two different clones growing near to one another if fruit is to be set.

When I was at school, the hymn for morning chapel, when a fine summer's day came along, would be changed (by Kenneth Stubbs, our music director) to a simple little one starting:

> So here hath been dawning another blue day,
> Say shall we let it slip useless away?
> Out of eternity this new day was born
> Back to eternity at night will return.

True blues may be few but I've given you enough for the dawning of many another blue day.

Agapanthus 'Loch Hope'
African blue lily
Height: 1.2m/4ft
Spread: 45cm/18in
Unreliably hardy, sun
Rich blue Headbourne hybrid with trumpet-shaped flowers on naked stems above a fountain of strap-like leaves. Mix with the strong yellows or oranges of kniphofias, crocosmias or cannas. *Lysimachia ciliata* 'Firecracker' looks good threading its way through blue agapanthus clumps.

Baptisia australis
False indigo
Height: 90cm/36in
Spread: 60cm/24in
Hardy, sun
Indigo blue, well spaced flowers in early summer, carried in elegant spikes, needing little more than a dark green background to show up the light green foliage. Drifts are better than single plants.

◄ Camassia cusickii
Quamash
Height: 90cm/36in
Spread: 20cm/8in
Hardy, sun
Spring-flowering North American bulb of easy cultivation in border or meadow. Becomes dormant soon after flowering. *C. quamash* is even more satisfactory as a meadow ingredient, making clumps with deep blue star flowers and self-sowing. Seeds ripen late summer.

Caryopteris x clandonensis
Height: 90cm/36in
Spread: 90cm/36in
Hardy, sun
With clusters of misty, blue flowers in terminal spires, and grey-green foliage, a shrub that mixes well with other late summer and autumn flowers, such as *Sedum* 'Herbstfreude'. *C. x c.* 'Worcester Gold' has yellow foliage which contrasts well with the deep blue flowers.

Ceanothus arboreus 'Trewithen Blue'
Californian lilac
Height: 6m/20ft
Spread: 6m/20ft
Hardy, sun
Early-flowering shrub, deep blue, with dark green rounded leaves. Good against brick walls, which offer some protection (it is susceptible to frosts), and with red rhododendrons.

Cerinthe major 'Purpurascens'
Height: 50cm/20in
Spread: 50cm/20in
Near-hardy, sun
Annual, best sown in autumn and overwintered under cold glass to plant out in spring. Long flowering season. Immensely popular because of unusual appearance, its blueness coming from glaucous leaves. Easily overrated.
▼

Chionodoxa luciliae
Glory of the snow
Height: 10cm/4in
Spread: 5cm/2in
Hardy, sun or light shade
Early-flowering bulb with wide-open starry flowers with a white centre. Good for naturalizing as long as there is not too much competition. Wonderful peeping through snow (hence the name), if it can be arranged.

Cynoglossum amabile ►
Chinese forget-me-not
Height: 60cm/24in
Spread: 30cm/12in
Hardy, sun
Annual or biennial bushy plant with light but bright blue flowers from early summer onwards. A sympathetic planting is with the blue lime grass, *Leymus arenarius*; for exciting contrast grow it with pot marigolds, *Calendula officinalis*.

Delphinium
Height: 2m/7ft
Spread: 75cm/30in
Hardy, sun
Spires of blue flowers of varying shades as well as whites, pinks, mauves and purples. Grow with the greenish-yellow *Cephalaria alpina*. The Belladonna hybrids go well with pink sidalcea or pale yellow *Thalictrum flavum* subsp. *glaucum*.

Eryngium x oliverianum
Sea holly
Height: 90cm/36in
Spread: 45cm/18in
Hardy, sun
Thistle-like plant with domed heads of flowers, surrounded by ruffs of prickly bracts, of an iridescent, metallic blue, including leaves and stem.

Echinops bannaticus 'Taplow Blue'
Globe thistle
Height: 1.2m/4ft
Spread: 60cm/2ft
Hardy, sun
Spherical flower heads of a bright blue, much loved by bees, held well above the very coarse leaves, which are best covered by a plant in front, leaving the flowers floating above it. Such a planting could include bright phloxes.

◀ *Geranium wallichianum* 'Buxton's Variety'
Height and spread: varies according to support
Hardy, partial shade
A rambling perennial that vanishes in winter and can be planted around with small, early bulbs like crocuses. Clambers into neighbours, flowering midsummer to late autumn. Colour a poor mauve in hot weather but steadily becoming bluer as it cools off.

Hosta 'Halcyon'
Height: 40cm/16in
Spread: 45cm/18in
Hardy, sun or light shade
Glaucous blue leaves that are relatively narrow and pointed. It has mauve flowers. 'Buckshaw Blue' has similar coloured leaves, but they are broader, and it has off-white flowers. Both are martyrs to slugs. Plant in front of the purplish foliage of *Rodgersia pinnata* 'Superba'.

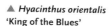

▲ *Hyacinthus orientalis* 'King of the Blues'
Height: 20cm/8in
Spread: 10cm/4in
Hardy, sun
An old hyacinth variety, fairly late-flowering, very deep blue and with an excellent, airborne fragrance. When planted out in the garden, this is very persistent, gradually building up a colony over the years.

***Hydrangea macrophylla* 'Générale Vicomtesse de Vibraye'**
Hortensia hydrangea
Height: 1m/40in
Spread: 1.2m/4ft
Hardy, light shade
On acid soils, rounded heads of a sky blue. Grow with the glaucous foliage of *Rosa glauca* and the purple plumes of *Astilbe chinensis* var. *taquetii* 'Superba'. Also good for containers, where soil acidity can be controlled with waterings of aluminium sulphate.

***Nigella damascena* 'Miss Jekyll'**
Love-in-a-mist
Height: 38cm/15in
Spread: 23cm/9in
Hardy, sun or light shade
Blue flowers with filigree-like appendages followed by inflated seed pods. An annual, it self-sows but should be thinned or potted up to get the best results. It flowers in late spring and early summer. As a contrast grow with calendula.

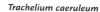

Polypodium aureum
Height: 50cm/20in
Width varies with age of plant, gradually spreading
Tender, full light or semi-shade
A handsome fern with the bluest fronds, simply pinnate or pinnatifid. Evergreen. Excellent for bedding out with contrasting tender perennials like foliage begonias. ◀

Salvia uliginosa
Bog sage
Height: 1.8m/6ft
Spread: 1m/40in
Hardy, sun
A tall, wiry plant with small spikes of white flecked, pale blue flowers held at the top of the swaying stems in the summer and autumn. It spreads. It may not be hardy in colder areas, so overwinter inside. Goes well with dahlias.

Trachelium caeruleum
Blue throatwort
Height: 30-60cm/12-24in
Spread: 30cm/12in
Tender, sun
Small pale blue flowers in a flat or dome-shaped head. The flowers are scented. Treat as an annual in frost-prone areas. It can be combined with another annual, *Gaillardia* 'Red Plume'.

***Veronica austriaca* subsp. *teucrium* 'Crater Lake Blue'**
Speedwell
Height: 45cm/18in
Spread: 30cm/12in
Hardy, sun
Spikes of deep blue flowers held above a mat of dull-green leaves, appearing from late spring to early summer. The flowering stems need some support. This perennial works well at the front of a border.

***Vinca minor* ▲**
Lesser periwinkle
Height: 8cm/3in
Spread: indefinite
Hardy, sun or shade
The most valuable ground-covering periwinkle. Flowers best in sun and most conspicuously if entire colony shorn back in late winter every other year. Typically coloured blue (especially 'La Grave').

The Value of MAUVE

Mauve as mauve has lost its popularity. But the fact that mauves and true blues do not associate well must never conceal their value to us with almost all other colours.

As a protagonist, mauve is seldom treated as a colour in its own right. Purple is and, of course, blue. But mauve flowers are either expected to masquerade as blue (campanula blue is mauve), lavender (a bluish mauve) or lilac (pinky-mauve). My idea of mauve at its most typical has always been *Iris unguicularis*, the winter-flowering Algerian iris, with its silky texture and surface sparkle.

Campanula blue, in particular, has singular freshness. Every early autumn, we sow a batch of biennial *Campanula patula* seed. The seedlings are brought on individually under cold glass and are planted out in early spring. They will carry airy sprays of mauve bellflowers for six weeks from early May. Everyone notices them and asks what they are, but none want to be bothered with a biennial. They miss so much. Naturally, you seldom want to think of a plant in isolation. A good companion for this campanula is the crimson ladybird poppy, raised and treated in the same way. The typical orange eschscholzia would also look good. To have it flowering early enough, it would need to have been sown the previous August. Old plants that have survived the winter also flower early.

The perennial *Campanula persicifolia* starts flowering in late May and is a great self-sower on heavy soils. But when I grow it deliberately and bed it out, I like to interplant a bronzy-brown

◀ Phlox paniculata, *the prototype of most of our summer-flowering border phloxes, is a tall, graceful plant, but in need of support. The domed panicle provides peaks and masses within the overall mass – eiderdowns of colour, often in two tones within the flower. Its other great asset is the scent, borne on the air and strongest while there is still dew around. I like it with the clear yellow of* Hemerocallis 'Marion Vaughn' (see page 82), *with the two groups intermingling a little at their adjacent margins.*

▲ Not so different in colour but completely different in habit and form: the biennial Campanula patula as a plinth for bulbous Allium hollandicum 'Purple Sensation' in late spring. This unusual bedding out arrangement will be swept aside a month later to make way for the next set piece.

▶ All campanula 'blue' is really mauve. Here, the tall, perennial Campanula lactiflora is seen through the gauze of clump-forming grass, Stipa gigantea. There is a nice spot, on top of a low retaining wall, on which to sit and rest and look at this.

Dutch bulbous iris. A similarly coloured iris is also a good interplant for the lilac-mauve, biennial wallflower, *Erysimum linifolium* (sown July-August and bedded out late autumn). So is the late-flowering tulip, 'Dillenburg', described in 'Orange'. The erysimum only gets into its stride mid-May.

One of the tallest campanulas, at 1.8m/6ft, is *C. lactiflora*, and that is usually mauve. It self-sows and I have a colony among July-flowering, pink hydrangeas, some of which are lacecaps, some hortensias. I couldn't have thought it out better (or as well) for myself. There is also a nearby plant of the 1.8m/6ft grass, *Stipa gigantea*, and I particularly like to seat myself on a low, flat-topped wall, nearby, so that I see the campanula through the rosy-tinted gauze of the grass in flower.

I have a lot of *Phlox paniculata*, prototype of the many cultivars it has given rise to, but far more graceful. Taller, too, at 1.2m/4ft and needing support. Its pure mauve colouring contrasts excellently with the sturdy, upright-growing *Astilbe chinensis* var. *taquetii* 'Superba', which is only a little shorter. It has narrow, spiky panicles of a really strong (almost brash) rosy-mauve. The contrast is not so much in colour but in their entirely different

shapes. Behind these two you could effectively grow the annual, purple form of orach, *Atriplex hortensis* (1.8m/6ft). As a substitute for *P. paniculata*, similar to it but having larger panicles, is 'Princess Sturdza'.

Another good companion for these mauve phloxes is *Hemerocallis* 'Marion Vaughn', one of the best American hybrids; it has outlived many more recent kinds in this competitive field. It is pale yellow and the fair-sized, well scented blooms jut forwards on the lower side. Like all day lilies of any size, it needs frequent dead-heading.

When you consider all the bright yellow perennials, especially sunflowers and other daisies, which flower in autumn, it is not surprising that the cool mauves of a range of perennial asters make soothing companions. They themselves will have yellow discs, so the contrast is already present. The August-flowering *Aster macrophyllus* (90cm/36in) is planted near to the front of my long border with the popular black-eyed Susan, *Rudbeckia fulgida* var. *sullivantii* 'Goldsturm', and they intermingle, the flowers at various levels, so there is no sense of uniformity and compactness as you find in the dwarfened *A. dumosus* hybrids.

Aster sedifolius flowers at about the same time, and that does make the densest of floral duvets, with spidery, interlocking daisies which you never see as units. Being top-heavy, it needs the securest brushwood support, put in quite early, but is worth the pains. What I love to grow near to it is the golden yellow crocosmia known by all of us as *C.* 'Citronella', though research would have 'Honey Angels' as correct. Its spear-leaves are an unusually bright shade of lime-green.

For a long season of flowering, from late July to October, *A.* x *frikartii* is unbeatable. Its daisies are quite sizeable but I find it a bit dull if used, as is so often the case, on its own. Opportunities of this kind are repeatedly frittered away. A fairly dwarf, pink Japanese anemone would be good or a deep crimson-leaved and -flowered annual *Amaranthus*, like the 'Red Fox' strain. As I regularly lose this aster to slugs, which devour its young shoots in spring before ever they surface, I have experimented with it less than I should wish.

The deep mauve *Verbena bonariensis* sows itself all over my garden and is a linking theme in certain areas. I have to control it pretty severely but, as I have said, it is one of those see-through plants that sometimes looks its best at a border's margin. It does not actually block the view to lower plants behind. I like this with

▲ *Accidental but none the less welcome: self-sown orach,* Atriplex hortensis var. rubra *behind the rather tall, late summer-flowering* Phlox maculata *'Princess Sturdza', growing in one of our stock beds.*

▶ *Mauves, but significantly and contrastingly backed and highlighted by the bamboo,* Phyllostachys bambusoides *'Castillonis'. Next comes purple* Atriplex hortensis var. rubra, *then* Phlox maculata *'Princess Sturdza', and, finally, in the foreground, the bold, upright panicles of brash mauve* Astilbe chinensis var. taquetii *'Superba'. It is supported by handsome, crimped foliage.*

▼ Hemerocallis *'Marion Vaughn' with* Phlox paniculata *in the Long Border, high summer. Phloxes love moisture but can be dashed by overhead spraying, so we administer a good soaking just before flowering starts and let that suffice.*

▲ A trickle of the tender, grey foliage plant, Plectranthus argentatus here separates the Michaelmas daisy, Aster 'Little Carlow', from black-eyed Rudbeckia fulgida var. deamii, both having a long, early autumn season.

▶ Two fairly short-lived but long-flowering perennials of similar habit: the greeny-yellow Patrinia scabiosifolia and mauve Verbena bonariensis. Each helps the other, colour-wise. Both are normally raised from seed. The patrinia's leaves are deeply divided but not much in evidence at flowering.

▼ Aster x frikartii 'Mönch' (60cm/24in) has a nearly three months-long season in late summer and early autumn. It contrasts well with bright pink Nerine bowdenii.

pale yellow, especially with *Patrinia scabiosifolia* (1.5m/5ft), which has heads of small, greeny-yellow flowers arranged in heads much like the verbena's own. The patrinia really prefers hotter summers than we can provide in order to set seed, which is the only practical method of increase and, like the verbena, it needs replacing every third year or so, as it is short-lived.

Another good companion for the verbena is the pale yellow Collerette dahlia, called 'Clair de Lune' (1.5m/5ft). I would say don't plant the verbena next to something as similar to itself as the much-loved *Thalictrum delavayi* (1.8m/6ft), with airy sprays of small mauve flowers. As I've said, it may be good taste but, at least for me, that is too subtle. A purple dahlia, like the Medium Cactus 'Hillcrest Royal', would be better as being more definite (which the verbena is not), yet still within the same colour band, if that is what you like.

Quite a different type of verbena, this time of the bedding-out persuasion, is the mauve 'La France' (30cm/12in). It has a spreading habit, which will weave into neighbours, even climbing a little, if they are taller than itself. I grew it in front of a strong yellow, black-coned *Rudbeckia hirta* hybrid, treated as an annual, called 'Indian Summer' (1.2m/4ft). There were white Japanese anemones behind them. Given an interval, I should like to repeat this. The verbena has quite fair-sized flower heads and it is scented.

A team of which I was proud, although the presence of self-sowns makes it partially accidental, not to say awkward to repeat, was, in April-May, a large clump of the elegant species *Gladiolus tristis* (90cm/36in), which is very pale yellow with a hint of green (lovely night scent), a late mauve tulip, 'Bleu Aimable', and the variegated honesty with disorganized cream variegation and mauve flowers (you may hate it; I am sorry for you). That is *Lunaria annua variegata* (not to be confused with another variegated honesty, *L.a.* 'Alba Variegata', with white flowers). It self-sows and if there are other plain-leaved *L. annua* around, they will spoil the strain and give rise to a preponderance of plain-leaved seedlings with flowers of unpredictable colouring.

One of our most valued annuals is *Ageratum* 'Blue Horizon'. This is a plant that Fergus enjoys threading through our borders and we never seem to raise enough of it. Unlike so many modern ageratum strains, which are dwarf and dense and do not age at all gracefully, 'Blue Horizon' grows to 60cm/24in, with a nice free habit and it flowers for several months with the minimum of

dead-heading. Its colour is not blue, but a great deal bluer than you ever see it in colour photographs. With pink Semperflorens begonias is nice, or with orange African marigolds.

Although we are all fascinated by the bluest of blue delphiniums, other colours also have their place and I particularly like a mauve Elatum hybrid called 'Mighty Atom'. It is by no means dwarf, but, at 1.5m/5ft a more convenient height for border integration than many modern cultivars. It looks nice in my long border with the flat-topped, very pale yellow *Achillea* 'Lucky Break' (90cm/36in) in front, the bright purple *Geranium* 'Ann Folkard' filtering through from one side and the powerful, lilac-mauve globes of self-sowing *Allium cristophii* (60cm/24in) scattered around. All this for a June to early July display.

A good mauve succession can be obtained with large candelabrums of biennial, June-July-flowering clary, *Salvia sclarea* var. *turkestanica*, interplanted with May-flowering *Allium hollandicum* (often listed as *A. aflatunense*) and infiltrated by self-sown, magenta-flowered *Lychnis coronaria* (both 90cm/36in). These will not last the summer through, so you can throw out the sage and lychnis in late July, harvest the allium bulbs and replant the whole area with, for instance, dahlias grown from late-struck cuttings, or with some strain of *Cosmos bipinnatus*, raised from a late May sowing. Or you could move in Michaelmas daisies or outdoor chrysanthemums which had been growing on in a stock bed. Given a good soak before and after the operation, they'll be perfectly amenable.

The soft-textured, fast-growing shrub, *Abutilon vitifolium*, with its May-flowering clusters of mauve, bowl-shaped flowers, is greatly improved in respect of intensity of colour, in the hybrid *A.* x *suntense*. I have thought how effective this would look hovering benignly over a generous colony of burnt-orange-flowered *Euphorbia griffithii* 'Fireglow'. I have twice been thwarted in the attempt. I have the spurge already established, but the abutilon quickly dies. It is liable to sudden death at the best of times, but there must be a fungus in the soil, here, that kills it off. I wish someone else would try. Too little thought is given to combining shrubs with perennials.

Although it hates my heavy soil, I cannot altogether ignore lavender, which typically comes in several shades of cool mauve. The July-flowering *Lavandula angustifolia* (in many cultivars) has the scent that suits it for lavender bags and that makes people pull off its flowering heads as they walk past a bush (and never mind

◀ *In a northwest-facing border, shaded till early afternoon, the yellow-leaved ivy,* Hedera helix *'Buttercup', has made a lively background for many changes of bedding, spring, summer and autumn and differing from year to year. Here, the mauve annual* Ageratum *'Blue Horizon' with pink and white fibrous-rooted, bedding begonias.*

▲ *White, yellow and mauve. The white Japanese* Anemone x hybrida *'Honorine Jobert' is a fixture. Our principal bedding-out area in front has annual* Rudbeckia *'Indian Summer' behind the tender perennial* Verbena *'La France'. This is sweetly scented and has the pleasant habit of weaving into its neighbours.*

▼ *A mauve Darwin tulip, its name long lost, has clumped up nicely since its original planting in the 1930s. Greeny-yellow leaves of* Symphytum *'Belsay' in the background.*

▲ *The mat-forming aubrietas of early spring are typically mauve. Here, on a retaining wall, they are in contrast with a self-sown spurge,* Euphorbia amygdaloides *var.* robbiae.

◄◄ *The Long Border in late June with spires of the not inconveniently tall, mauve* Delphinium *'Mighty Atom'. Later we try to mask its remains with an annual climber like morning glory,* Ipomoea *(syn.* Mina) lobata *or* Rhodochiton atrosanguineus. *In front, the pale yellow yarrow,* Achillea *'Lucky Break', and long-flowering cranesbill,* Geranium *'Ann Folkard', which is brightest purple with a black eye. A froth of white annual (but sown the previous autumn)* Ammi majus, *later to be replaced with another tall annual, perhaps* Cosmos bipinnatus *'Purity' or* Tithonia rotundifolia *'Torch'.*

▶ *More mauve retaining-wall aubrietas. Quite a spring meeting, here, with the bright pinky-mauve* Bergenia stracheyi, Narcissus cyclamineus *hybrid 'Jetfire' and some primroses. These are all planted (the primrose self-sown) in the flat ground above the wall.*

how nasty the remaining, decapitated stalks look). Roses of a clear pink colouring do go especially well with lavenders of this kind. The square-headed French lavender, *L. stoechas,* is already in full bloom in May, and has a rather different scent. And there are a number of tender species, among which I am fond of *L. dentata,* fast-growing, with deckle-edged leaves and pale mauve flowers over a long season. Hardly showy, yet endearing.

And what shall we say of lilac, *Syringa vulgaris?* A big, ungainly bush, and yet indispensable. Lilac Time says it all; the scent and the stamp of spring. Of course there are many desirable improved variants, purple, white, double, heavy-headed, but the unimproved lilac lilac is a great survivor, often seen around rubbish dumps in the same way as elder. I love to see, probably in some suburban garden, the exuberant combination of lilac, laburnum (as yellow as can be) and double pink or red may (hawthorn). And I don't want to hear so much as a whisper of that word vulgar.

One of the first crocuses of the new year is the slim little mauve *Crocus tommasinianus* and that contrasts excitingly with the rich orange *C. flavus,* when both are grown in a meadow setting. We need all the excitement we can muster in February. Another good combination is *C. tommasinianus* with yellow winter aconites, *Eranthis hyemalis.* They will even thrive under a beech tree, which is one of the most difficult sites, in summer, because of the darkness and drowth there. But in winter there is moisture and light. The bluest of all crocuses, albeit still mauve, is the autumn-flowering *C. speciosus,* and that will spread into a fair-sized colony under meadow conditions. The best, though unpremeditated, contrast I had for that was where it grows just outside the perimeter of my favourite hawthorn, *Crataegus laciniata.* Its large orange haws ripen in September and are bowed by their weight to the ground, just where the crocus is flowering.

Typical aubrieta is mauve as they come, and so generous; as happy in a retaining wall as on the flat. I have a sneaking *penchant* for the interplanting of that with a little (not too much) of the exceedingly bright mustard yellow *Alyssum saxatile,* now changed to *Aurinia saxatilis.* Anyway, you are certainly familiar with the plant I mean. Another good combination with which I have played, where aubrieta anyway grows in big pads on the face of a retaining wall, is with *Bergenia stracheyi* on the ledge just above it. That has neat little leaves and an abundance of rosy-magenta blossom in tight clusters, late March to early April.

I hope I have now made an excellent case for mauve.

Abutilon x suntense
Height: 3m/10ft
Spread: 2.4m/8ft
Hardy, sun
A loose shrub with saucer-shaped to flat flowers of a rich, deep mauve. It will survive winter outside, but must have well-drained soil to do this. Plant it so that the flowers appear above the burnt-orange-flowered *Euphorbia griffithii* 'Fireglow'.

Ageratum 'Blue Horizon'
Floss flower
Height: 60cm/24in
Spread: 30cm/12in
Tender, sun
Taller and freer growing than most modern strains, this variety bears mauve flowers for most of the summer and into autumn, without need of dead-heading. Plant out after frosts, with *Cleome pungens,* pink Semperflorens begonias or, for a stronger contrast, with orange African marigolds or *Rudbeckia* 'Indian Summer'.

Allium cristophii
Height: 60cm/24in
Spread: 23cm/9in
Hardy, sun
One of the largest-headed alliums with small star-like mauve flowers held on long stalks forming a sphere. It self-sows and crops up elsewhere in the garden. It dries well. Other tall and imposing alliums, all mauve, are 'Beau Regard', 'Globemaster', 'Gladiator' and 'Lucy Ball'.
◄

Aster sedifolius
Height: 90cm/36in
Spread: 60cm/24in
Hardy, sun
A loose, flopping plant (needing support) with dense heads containing masses of daisy flowers with mauve petals and a yellow disc, appearing in late summer and early autumn. Grow trails of bright nasturtiums through it or mix it with *Crocosmia* 'Citronella'.

Aster x frikartii
Height: 90cm/36in
Spread: 60cm/24in
Hardy, sun
One of the best asters, this has large flowers with mauve petals and a yellow disc. It flowers over a long period from midsummer well into autumn. Grow it with pink Japanese anemones or the deep crimson-leaved and -flowered annual *Amaranthus*.

Aubrieta
Height: 5cm/2in
Spread: 60cm/24in
Hardy, sun
A mat-forming perennial with low growing, flat flowers in spring. The common form is mauve, although there are variants from pink to purple. It can be grown in or over walls and rock gardens as well as on the flat. A plant for a similar situation is the virulent yellow *Aurinia saxatilis (Alyssum saxatile)* which can be mixed with it in moderation.

Campanula lactiflora
Milky bellflower
Height: 1.8m/6ft
Spread: 60cm/24in
Hardy, sun or light shade
A tall perennial campanula with a bold display of mauve bellflowers in early to midsummer. It self-sows around, producing slight colour variation. It looks good with pink Lacecap and Hortensia hydrangeas.

Campanula patula
Spreading bellflower
Height: 60cm/24in
Spread: 60cm/24in
Hardy, sun
A delightful airy biennial with floating small to medium-sized mauve bells, a bit like a larger harebell. It flowers over a long period in late spring and early summer. Try it with eschscholzias or *Papaver commutatum*.
▼

Crocus tommasinianus
Height: 10cm/4in
Spread: 5cm/2in
Hardy, sun or light shade
A delightful crocus that seems almost invisible until the flowers open, when they are a definite shade of mauve, sometimes purple. It readily self-sows and can be naturalized, along with the rich orange *C. flavus*.
◄
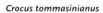

Erysimum linifolium
Wallflower
Height: 30cm/12in
Spread: 25cm/10in
Hardy, sun
A very short-lived perennial wallflower, best treated as a biennial. The flowers are mauve and open a little later than most wallflowers. It goes well with the late-flowering, orange and pink tulip 'Dillenburg' and later in the season *Phlox paniculata*.

Hepatica nobilis
Height: 10cm/4in
Spread: 20cm/8in
Hardy, light shade
A woodland plant needing humus-rich soil whose mauve-blue flowers twinkle out from the shade during the late winter and early spring, when there is little else around. It fits in well with the purples of *Cyclamen coum*. There are other colours including deep rosy pink that is almost red.

Iris unguicularis
Winter iris
Height: 30cm/12in
Spread: 60cm/24in
Hardy, sun
This iris with pure mauve flowers is a non-stop delight from November to March. The flowers are a martyr to slugs and caterpillars. Best planted in a sunny spot in poor, well-drained soil next to a wall where it needs no other companions at this time of year.
▼

Lavandula stoechas subsp. **pedunculata 'James Compton'**
Lavender
Height: 60cm/24in
Spread: 60cm/24in
Hardy, sun
Members of this species are markedly square in section, the flowers aligned on the four corners and crowned with a flag-like bunch of mauve bracts. They flower late spring – far earlier than English lavenders. The flower head sits only just above the foliage, but in this subspecies the stalk is long. ▶

Lunaria annua variegata
Variegated honesty
Height: 90cm/36in
Spread: 30cm/12in
Hardy, sun or light shade
With mauve flowers and cream variegated foliage, this biennial honesty illuminates a shady spot. If not dead-headed, it will self-sow and become a permanent feature. Good with the late mauve tulip 'Bleu Aimable' and pale yellow *Gladiolus tristis*.
▼

Phlox paniculata
Border phlox
Height: 1.2m/4ft
Spread: 30cm/12in
Hardy, sun
With soft mauve flowers carried in graceful, airy heads, the species is taller and simpler in colour than many of its cultivars. It needs discreet staking in exposed gardens. Good with *Astilbe chinensis taquetii* 'Superba' in front and the purple *Atriplex hortensis* behind.

Salvia sclarea var. turkestanica
Biennial clary
Height: 1.2m/4ft
Spread: 45cm/18in
Hardy, sun
A biennial with large spikes of white and mauve flowers that look quite papery at a distance. Try planting it with the purple *Allium hollandicum* and the vivid, magenta-flowered *Lychnis coronaria*.

Solanum crispum 'Glasnevin'
Chilean potato tree
Height: 6m/20ft
Spread: 4m/13ft
Hardy, sun
A large, loose shrub covered with clear mauve flowers, held in loose heads, from late spring through to the autumn. Plant it against a wall or as a free-standing shrub, perhaps with the yellow-flowered *Cytisus battandieri*.
▶

Verbena bonariensis
Height: 1.8m/6ft
Spread: 30cm/12in
Hardy, sun
Tall, wiry stems and heads of mauve-purple flowers from late June to November. A short-lived perennial, it readily self-sows in well-drained soil. It combines with many plants but is especially good with the pale yellow *Patrinia scabiosifolia*.
▶

Enigmatic GREEN

Green is the colour of life. No green, no life.
We take it for granted but are enigmatic in our
interpretation of its significance.

◄ *Some people are put off*
by the almost animal-like
energy of unfurling fern
fronds in spring. They
should revel in this. One of
the brightest, on its first
appearance, is the
colonizing shuttlecock fern,
Matteuccia struthioperis.
It is best in a cool climate,
scorching in summer if too
hot or dry.

Red for danger; green for safety, and yet the commonest form of colour blindness cannot distinguish between the two. Not much safety in that.

Green wood is raw and unseasoned and we apply this condition to our own inexperience. Shakespeare's Cleopatra spoke of 'my salad days when I was green in judgement'. But green also stands for all that is good and desirable in our environment and opposed to its blighting and pollution by the presence and activities of mankind.

In temperate climates, where rain is plentiful, green is everywhere. But as soon as you reach hotter, drier regions, green is at a premium. Rich property owners will insist on having green lawns, even though the greener grasses may detest the conditions and will go down to a range of fungal diseases. In countries like Britain, where grass is abundant and deciduous trees the norm, the huge surge of bright green new foliage in spring may easily make the countryside more attractive than our own gardens. We can drive around in a heated car, admiring the scene, whereas exposed in a garden, it is easy to be numbingly cold. But late in the summer, it is the other way round and plants that remain bright green through to autumn should be held in high esteem.

However bright, green is soothing. It does not dazzle, in the way that blocks of red, orange, yellow or white easily could. So it

▲ *One of the best hardy perennials for cooling off a mixture of hot colours, in summer, is* Helianthus salicifolius *(at back), with columns of narrow leaves.*

▼ *Perhaps the best foliage shrub for bright, glistening green is* x Fatshedera lizei, *a cross between ivy and* Fatsia japonica. *It can grow to 2m/7ft but has a lax habit and I cut it quite hard all over each spring.*

▶ *A border largely shaded by our house. For a foreground, the late Dutch honeysuckle has several interestingly green plants: the big heart leaves of* Clerodendrum bungei, *which flowers in autumn; the symmetry of* Paris polyphylla, *which is green all through and remains in shape from late May to October; and the spurge,* Euphorbia x martinii, *with excellent foliage and long-lasting flower heads.*

acts as a buffer and can be used to separate warring colours. It is the linking motto colour *par excellence*.

One concept of a minimalist garden is that all the plants should be green. I should enjoy making that. The hard landscaping could include whitewashed walls (though not dead white), terracotta tiles, restrained paving, and I would allow no lawns. The plants' principal importance would then be concentrated on their shapes and textures, and on their different shades of calming green. Shadows would play an important role. The shadows of bamboos on walls and paving, for instance. Or of the big, glossy, fingered leaves of a big shrub like *Fatsia japonica*. In fact, I have such an area in my own, walled garden, although it is in shade for most of the day. Near to the fatsia, the hybrid between itself and ivy called x *Fatshedera lizei*. This is a lax, non-climbing shrub with brightest green, largish ivy-like leaves. And on the wall behind these is an actual ivy, the rather large-leaved *Hedera colchica* 'Dentata Variegata', which is variegated in cream and two shades of green.

Lacy ferns make an ideal contrast to bold shapes like the above ivy relatives and I have several of them, not all together but among contrasting ingredients. Boldest is a big clump of *Polystichum setiferum* 'Pulcherrimum Bevis' (90cm/36in), in which the twice-divided (bipinnate) fronds are drawn to a long, closed-up tip. That is semi-evergreen, needing to be cut back only at winter's end. Whereas the gossamer-light, finely divided lady fern, *Athyrium filix-femina* 'Plumosum Axminster' is deciduous and incredibly fresh in spring. The main contrasting neighbour to that is a colony of an exceptional, deciduous perennial, *Paris polyphylla* (60cm/24in). Each naked stem is crowned first by a whorl of about nine lance leaves, which form a framing ruff; then further, smaller whorls of its floral parts, still green; finally a purplish knob, which is the flower's developing seed capsule. This structure is maintained right through from May to October, when the capsule opens to reveal a nest of brilliant orange seeds.

Behind these is a shiny-leaved, evergreen shrub, of graceful form to 1.8m/6ft, *Sarcococca ruscifolia*. Other supporting plants include *Tellima grandiflora*, with scalloped leaves. It rises to 60cm/24in when its sprays of green flowers are out in spring. And there is a small colony of the near evergreen perennial, *Epimedium pinnatum* subsp. *colchicum* (30cm/12in), whose ground-covering foliage, coppery when young, is its main point, although the yellow flowers in spring are nice. Among and

▲ *One of our handsomest ferns, almost year-round, is Polystichum setiferum 'Pulcherrimum Bevis' (many ferns are burdened with long names). Here it is rubbing cheeks with Spiraea japonica 'Goldflame'.*

▼ *The almost evergreen fern, Polypodium interjectum 'Cornubiense', is at its brightest in winter and contrasts well with the young marbled foliage of Arum italicum subsp. italicum 'Marmoratum'. Another good association is with the scarlet berries of the hermaphrodite form of butcher's broom, Ruscus aculeatus. All are happy in shade.*

between these plants I have the Viridiflora tulip, 'Spring Green', in pale and darker green, and surprisingly lively.

In front of the 'Bevis' fern, I am establishing one of my favourite hardy foliage plants for shady places: *Asarum europaeum*. It makes a low cushion of dark green, almost circular leaves with a scintillating gloss on them, so that even beneath a canopy of trees, any light reaching it is cheerfully reflected.

There is nothing remotely boring about this quiet corner and I often stop appreciatively to take it in. Green is not there merely as an unavoidable necessity; it is, in this and many cases, a protagonist. I have to admit that in the area just described, I do include some flowering plants – hellebores, snowdrops, pulmonarias – but then I am a plantsman. I am great at making rules for others and breaking them for myself.

If you enjoy ferns, nearly all of which are green, you will find yourself collecting them. Don't herd them all together; there is too great a similarity in the feathery construction of the fronds, in most cases (the plain straps of hart's tongue ferns is the obvious exception). Contrast them with plants enjoying similar damp and partly shaded conditions but having a different style in foliage. Hostas, with their broad, undivided leaves, come immediately to mind. Arums, also.

Arums have beautiful, glossy spear-shaped (hastate) leaves. One of the most popular, grown almost entirely for its foliage (although its club-shaped, orange fruit structures in August come as an unexpected surprise) is *Arum italicum* subsp. *italicum* 'Marmoratum'. Its veins are highlighted in pale green, while the body of the leaf is dark green. This appears on the scene from October and lasts through to May, when it aestivates, like many plants from warmer countries. *Arum creticum*, from Crete, is another such – at its lushest in late winter and early spring, when its glossy foliage stands out with attractively sharp angular outlines. Its dramatic yellow flowers are borne in April – only for a few days but such a concentrated feast that it seems far longer.

Of the arum family is *Arisaema*, which are fascinating hardy perennials though slow to propagate and not always easily obtainable. The spathe forms a hood, is often green or striped green and, at the top, frequently ends in a long tail. But the long-lasting foliage is of even greater significance. In *A. consanguineum* (60cm/24in), for instance, the leaflets are spread in a fan about an arc and they are mottled in two shades of green.

The florist's arum or calla lily, *Zantedeschia aethiopica*, is a

◄ Few plants are so well suited by their foliage as the florist's arum Zantedeschia aethiopica, which makes the ideal foil to the arum's white spathes.

▼ Sustaining all winter: the patterned foliage of Cyclamen hederifolium with a wavy-margined form (Crispum Group) of our native hart's tongue fern, Asplenium scolopendrium.

▼ The little adder's tongue fern, Ophioglossum vulgatum, is deciduous but should be looked out for in old meadow turf, in spring. It makes colonies but hates disturbance.

◄ This hardy papyrus, Cyperus vegetus (syn. C. eragrostis), sowed itself into a carpet of Juniperus sabina 'Tamariscifolia'. It has an interesting and unusual shape, but cannot be allowed to spread everywhere, or else it looks weedy.

▲ *The ground-covering, non-climbing* Clematis x jouiniana *'Praecox' is a bit flat and featureless on its own, but is here given a lift by neighbouring columns of* Helianthus salicifolius, *with bamboo* Phyllostachys nigra f. punctata *making a green cloud behind.* Buddleja davidii *'Dartmoor' behind that.*

▼ *The evergreen shrub* Itea ilicifolia *rains green every August, with long tassels of blossom, honey-scented at night. Nobody fails to notice it.*

▶ *Although I believe a mixed border should include plenty of heavyweights, it also needs a leavening contrast, which the summer-flowering tamarisk,* Tamarix ramosissima, *achieves all summer and autumn, with tiny pale green leaves, only erupting into a haze of pink blossom in August. Cardoons,* Cynara cardunculus, *are flowering behind.*

weed in its native South Africa, cattle always avoiding it, but such a sight in early spring, its white spathes (which I shall come back to in the next chapter) held proudly as a lesson in deportment and perfectly set off by its sculptural dark green foliage. There is a cultivar called 'Green Goddess', in which most of the spathe is green. It is beloved of flower arrangers but passes for nothing on the plant, because green flowers do not show up among green leaves.

When the brightest section (the top third) of my long border is at its most colourful peak, in July, the greens in it remain vital. A large, tree-like *Gleditsia triacanthos* 'Elegantissima' blocks out any view of the house (you see that dominantly from other parts of the border) and thus creates a feeling of enclosure and intimacy. It leafs out late in May and is a fresh shade of green all summer, with pinnate foliage.

There is an airy duo of summer-flowering tamarisk, *Tamarix ramosissima*, contributing lightness in contrast to heavy hydrangeas and border phloxes. Itself changes to pink, when flowering in August. *Helianthus salicifolius*, at 1.8m/6ft or so (the height varies) has distinguished columns of narrow, drooping, green foliage right through to its flowering time in late September. It here acts as an admirable break between yellow mulleins with *Senecio doria* behind, and a pink phlox in front. The 'Lochinch' buddleja at the back of the border has not yet started flowering but is grey-green in the run-up, while another back-of-border shrub which contributes year-round is a silvery green cherry-laurel, *Prunus laurocerasus* 'Castlewellan' (5m/15ft).

A large, though broken, mound of rather dusty grey-green Jerusalem sage, *Phlomis fruticosa* (1.2m/4ft), tones down the bright pinks and mauves of phloxes, which crowd in on it from every side. As soon as they start flowering, we remove the tired yellow flower heads from the sage, though they were good through June. I have had this veteran since 1950 and have no intention of pensioning it off.

What shall we say about the claim that well-kept lawns are the ideal setting for colourful borders? The alternative is paving, which can be awful; lawns are at least safe and predictable. But good paving is immensely satisfying, making the right contrast for almost any colour. Furthermore, it allows plants to surge forwards from where they were planted, which gives an air of contentment and relaxation to the scene. Surging forwards over grass will kill the grass. Paving does not have to look stodgy or uniform, whereas turf, composed of bitty little grass blades, inevitably does.

▲ Most euphorbias have green flowers of a lively shade contrasting with their leaves. They have good bold shapes and so feature frequently in this book. Euphorbia schillingii (1.2m/4ft) is a clump-forming perennial that flowers from early July into September. It is a good mixer.

◄◄ In the Exotic Garden's peak season, leaf shapes and colouring are all-important. Dominant here is the shrubby Tetrapanax papyrifer (on the left), the grass Miscanthus sinensis 'Variegatus' (back centre), the New Zealand flax, Phormium 'Sundowner', striped pink and green, and right at back the huge heart-shaped leaves of a heavily pruned Paulownia tomentosa. Luxuriance is my aim.

Mown grass is featureless, flat and boring. In a park or public garden, it is the cheapest form of area management but, apart from being green, it has no appeal. A meadow area, mown perhaps just twice a year, is entirely different. There's shadow and movement; the grasses bend before the wind and the light catches and reflects from their stems. Then there can be a range of grass species, each with its own character and each flowering in its season. The appearance of a meadow is constantly changing. You can add other kinds of plants to it. Red clover, in May, never looks so bright as in a setting of vivid green grass.

As spring moves into summer, green foliage that was so bright when young settles down, in most cases, to solemn middle age. In many trees – beeches and elms, for instance – it becomes really heavy. We are then particularly grateful for those exceptions which retain a lively colouring.

Among trees, the pinnate leaves of false acacia, *Robinia pseudoacacia*, always remain light and cheerful and the swamp cypress, *Taxodium distichum*, retains a spring-like freshness right up to the time, in autumn, when it takes on the foxy tints for which its fall dress is famed. One cannot help comparing it with the dawn redwood, *Metasequoia*, which is another deciduous conifer with pinnate foliage. But that is an unremarkable green, in summer. It is much faster growing, which may or may not be an advantage. Taxodiums make beautiful old trees. *Metasequoia* has not been with us for long enough to judge.

Among border plants, two, both tender perennials with lively green needle leaves, have come into circulation quite recently. *Eupatorium capillifolium* is tall (1.8m/6ft by the end of the summer) and narrow; *Artemisia capillaris* is shorter (1.2m/4ft) and broader. Both are an admirable break to bright colours. They should be grouped, not dotted singly – an arrangement which generally looks self-conscious. Neither appears to flower, unless right at the end of the season and then insignificantly. Both can be propagated in autumn from cuttings, overwintered under frost-free glass.

The so-called burning bush or summer cypress, *Bassia* (syn. *Kochia*) *scoparia* f. *trichophylla* (1.5m/5ft), is an annual making a neat cone of brightest green, linear foliage. In formal bedding it can look dreadfully self-conscious, because of its outline, but I like it a lot, making a totally informal group in a mixed border, and it contrasts strikingly with the richest orange African marigolds (*Tagetes erecta*). In September, the bassia changes (disconcertingly, unless you're ready for it) to brilliant magenta. There is a strain

▲ *I often use a well-curled parsley in my bedding as the colour is such a lively shade of green through late summer and autumn. Orange, as with marigolds here, contrasts strikingly.*

called 'Evergreen', but it isn't; it changes to magenta like the rest.

A nicely crimped, mossy strain of parsley (*Petroselinum*), such as 'Bravour', is especially lively in a bedding-out or mixed border setting in late summer and autumn (in early summer I find that too many plants are killed by virus infection, turning to pink as they die). With this I like to contrast an orange strain of *Tagetes tenuifolia*, like 'Starfire' (30cm/12in) which makes mounds of countless quite tiny daisies. The single-flowered, dwarf orange French marigold *T. patula* 'Disco Orange' also works well.

If we thought more about green in our gardening plans, we should be better in-depth gardeners. With Fergus, driving home across a flood valley one sunny midday in winter, I was struck by the joyful contrast made by blue floodwater and sky, green meadow grass around the flood margins, and white seagulls sitting around everywhere. Why not a green, blue and white planting, I thought? I am still working on that one. You know how it is in gardening; I was immediately thwarted because the white phlox that I used turned out to have a soil-borne fungal disease, verticillium wilt. Not only did it have to go but we had to sterilize the ground in the two areas where it grew, which takes time. The green element was *Helianthus salicifolius*; the blue, delphiniums. Now I must think of some suitable white-flowered plant that will coincide with the delphiniums. I shall record the result if and when it works. With plants at least, one must be patient.

Green is a protagonist as well as a background and we shouldn't underestimate it. In our adventurous borders the loudest reds or oranges, with which it contrasts so tellingly, can be let loose given green as a safety net.

Arisaema consanguineum
Height: up to 60cm/24in
Spread: 20cm/8in
Hardy, shade
Long-lasting foliage, mottled in two shades of green, and curious green-hooded flowers, striped dandily with white, on purple-mottled stems. Grow with other foliage plants that like cool, leafy soil.
◄

Arum italicum 'Marmoratum'
Italian arum
Height: 30cm/12in
Spread: 30cm/12in
Hardy, shade or sun
Grown for its winter and spring foliage which is arrow shaped, green with silvery-green markings along the veins. In late summer and autumn it produces spikes of orange red berries. Good for planting under hedges or shrubs.

Artemisia capillaris
Height: 1.2m/4ft
Spread: 45cm/18in
Tender, sun
Bright green foliage with insignificant flowers, this tender perennial can be used for individual focal points, but is best grouped.

Asarum europaeum ▶

Wild ginger
Height: 15cm/6in
Spread: 30cm/12in
Hardy, shade
A perennial that forms carpets in shady and woodland settings, preferring non-alkaline soil. The round, dark glossy green leaves have a shine which reflects light. Plant with the fern *Athyrium niponicum* var. *pictum* which has grey fronds or winter aconites.

Athyrium filix-femina 'Plumosum Axminster'
Lady fern
Height: 90cm/36in
Spread: 1.2m/4ft
Hardy, shade
A deciduous lacy fern of great delicacy which is at its best in the spring, beginning to look tired in September. It can be planted next to other green plants such as *Paris polyphylla*, or contrasted with orange or yellow Welsh poppies, *Meconopsis cambrica*, which will help illuminate dark corners. 'Minutissimum' is a lady fern in miniature.

Bassia (syn. Kochia) scoparia f. trichophylla
Burning bush
Height: up to 1.5m/5ft
Spread: 45cm/18in
Tender, sun
An old-fashioned bedding annual, also known as *Kochia*, which forms a dense cone of fine green foliage that suddenly changes to magenta in the autumn. A group can be used as a green element in a border or contrasted with the rich oranges of African marigolds.

Eupatorium capillifolium
Dog fennel
Height: 2m/7ft
Spread: 30cm/12in
Tender, sun
An upright plant with hairy stems producing deeply cut, light green foliage which stays fresh into October. The flowers are insignificant. The columns of green can be used to separate colours in a border. It is best planted in groups.

Euphorbia palustris ▲
Spurge
Height: 60cm/24in plus; taller after flowering
Spread: splaying outwards to 1m/40in
Hardy, sun or part shade
Herbaceous spurge, that never needs disturbing. Loves heavy, moist soil. Freshest lime-green inflorescences in late spring. Combines well with blue, orange, red or white.

◄ **Farfugium japonicum 'Aureomaculatum'**
Height (foliage only): 25cm/10in
Spread: 40cm/16in
Semi-tender, light shade
Farfugiums do not flower in the cool summers of Britain. Splendid foliage plants, they like moist, organically rich soil. The plain-leaved prototype is as handsome as any. This yellow-spotted form is excellent if you don't hate it. 'Argenteum' is boldly segmented with white.

Gleditsia triacanthos 'Elegantissima'
Honey locust
Height: 6m/20ft
Spread: 5m/16ft
Hardy, sun
A shrubby tree with attractive pinnate foliage which has a fern-like quality. It maintains its fresh-looking green throughout the summer. The leaves turn yellow in the autumn. Unlike other cultivars, this one is thornless.

Helianthus salicifolius
Willow-leaved sunflower
Height: 1.8m/6ft
Spread: 1m/40in
Hardy, sun
The narrow, willow-type leaves droop slightly, covering the long stem from top to bottom. In a plant's early stages, it closely resembles a lily before flowering, for which it is often confused. A group forms a wonderful green break in a flowery border. In winter, the old stems take on interesting greyish tones.

Helleborus argutifolius ▲
Corsican hellebore
Height: 40cm/16in
Spread: 60cm/24in
Hardy, damp, light shade
Semi-shrubby, evergreen hellebore with leaves trifoliate edged with mock prickles. Long, spring-flowering season, pale green in bunches. Renews itself annually from the base. Also self-sows.

Matteuccia struthiopteris
Shuttlecock fern
Height: 1m/40in
Spread: indefinite
Hardy, damp shade (scorches in sun)
Deciduous fern, at its freshest in spring, with light green fronds arranged in shuttlecock-shaped rings. Rapidly outward-spreading into colonies.

Paris polyphylla ▶
Height: 90cm/36in
Spread: 30cm/12in
Hardy, light shade
A plant of arresting structure in which most of its parts, including the flower, are green. It can be used where contrasting shapes are needed, such as with ferns. It emerges late, so do not accidentally dig it up or plant on top of it.

Phlomis fruticosa
Jerusalem sage
Height: 1.2m/4ft
Spread: 1.2m/4ft
Hardy, sun
A sprawling shrub with dusty grey-green leaves, which has whorls of golden labiate flowers in early summer. Underplant with violets and snowdrops. Remove the dead flowering stems.

Polystichum setiferum 'Pulcherrimum Bevis'
Soft shield fern
Height: 90cm/36in
Spread: 75cm/30in
Hardy, light shade
A beautiful feathery fern with twice divided fronds. It is evergreen but remove old foliage in spring to make way for new. It goes well with *Spiraea japonica* 'Goldflame'.

Prunus laurocerasus 'Castlewellan'
Cherry laurel
Height: 5m/16ft
Spread: 5m/16ft
Hardy, sun or light shade
An evergreen back-of-border shrub with shiny mid-green leaves splashed with silvery-white. It has spikes of white flowers in spring.

Tamarix ramosissima
Tamarisk
Height: 3m/10ft
Spread: 3m/10ft
Hardy, sun
Arching stems of tiny leaves and light, airy sprays of pink flowers in late summer make a good contrast with hydrangeas and border phloxes.

Taxodium distichum
Swamp cypress
Height: 40m/130ft
Spread: 10m/33ft
Hardy, sun
Eventually a tall tree, but slow-growing and remaining narrow. The deciduous, soft foliage is a very fresh green, retained until it takes on russet autumn tints.

◀ **Tulipa 'Spring Green'**
Height: 40cm/16in
Spread: 15cm/6in
Hardy, sun
A late-flowering tulip of the Viridiflora type. The flowers are a loose cup shape, ivory, greenish white in colour with darker green markings. Good with lime-green *Smyrnium perfoliatum* or *Tellima grandiflora*.

Broken WHITE

A great burden of unsullied purity is borne by the colour white. Cold, staring and assertive, it draws your eye but makes you wish it hadn't.

◀ A single white daisy demonstrates the advantage of its contrasting yellow eye. Had it been entirely double and all white, we should have been made uncomfortable. The moon daisy or ox-eyed daisy, Leucanthemum vulgare (45cm/18in), is a beautiful component in meadow turf. It also colonizes paving cracks, making a generous display from late May for three or four weeks.

White is not a generous colour, taking more than it gives. It is the colour of ice and snow and a denial that life continues. It was always the colour of funeral flowers. Now, no longer, but the feeling that white flowers are funereal dies hard in many less sophisticated communities.

The purifying, virginal implication of white also persists in white weddings. It was traditional to include white myrtle blossom in a bride's bouquet, and lucky to own a plant that had been struck from a cutting taken from the bouquet. My own myrtle bush, *Myrtus communis*, planted before I was born, was, my mother told me, a cutting from a cutting in a wedding bouquet. Whose bouquet, I unfortunately forget!

Most white flowers include softening, mitigating elements. Snowdrops follow snow-melt but are not in the least frigid themselves. Their petals are curved, catching the light in many different ways. There is green in their bells and the whole flower is elegantly poised, so that it dances to air movements. Snowdrops open and close in response to warmth and chill. They are fragrant and are eagerly visited for early nectar by bees. These are altogether joyful flowers, heralds of spring before its actual arrival.

Gardeners in general are mesmerized by white. They know that it is considered a respectable colour, over whose use no one would dream of criticizing them, yet they understandably find it

hard to handle. So they create white gardens and white borders but exclude white from general plantings. But in small doses rather than cold, solid blocks, white has a magical luminosity that seems to beckon you towards it.

Fergus and I are very fond of a June-flowering border phlox, *Phlox carolina* 'Miss Lingard' (1m/40in), for its neat, rounded flowers and its shapely, elongated inflorescence. Slightly over-excited, we planted a huge swathe of it, admittedly in a nursery stock bed, not primarily intended for display, siting a deep mauve phlox near to it and a large amount of the scarlet, dome-headed *Lychnis chalcedonica*. But the phlox was so unremittingly white that it seemed to attack your vision like a blunderbuss. Had we planted just a single clump of the tall, spraying grass, *Stipa gigantea*, in front, and at the junction of the three just mentioned, it would, at that season, have been creating a diaphanous veil of rose-tinted, oat-like flower heads, seen through which the phlox would have appeared like a stage set, seen at one remove, through a gauze curtain.

So white should take its place in general plantings. Not, as I've said, in blocks, but dispersed. 'Miss Lingard', for instance, could well be used several times over and in the same general area, but separated and perhaps only as single clumps, yet emotionally and visibly connected as an interrupted theme, sometimes brought a little forward, sometimes receding. It might not be just 'Miss Lingard', but include other white flowers.

Many white flowers are tiny units with gaps between them but assembled into huge, airy clouds of blossom. In a pear tree, each cloud is quite small and dense, but there are great quantities of them, all exhaling a powerful, somewhat sickly but wholly characteristic fragrance. *Ammi majus* (sown in autumn and brought on in pots, 1.8m/6ft) has umbels of pure white with a wonderful lightness that contrasts well with columns of willowy *Helianthus salicifolius*. *Gypsophila paniculata* is a cloud of tiny units, while *Crambe cordifolia* (2.4m/8ft), is sheer dissipated white with the sparkle of a firework. The hardy perennial *Sanguisorba tenuifolia* 'Alba' (90cm/36in) dangles a hover of pussy-tails, consisting mainly of powderpuff stamens. An underplanting of the crimson, black-centred poppy, *Papaver commutatum* 'Ladybird', to flower in June, described in 'Red' on page 17, is dramatic enough to cite again.

White flowers often have an inbuilt leavening of yellow at their centre. It may be their stamens, as in the Madonna lily, *Lilium*

▲ Snowdrops and snow may correspond in time but are entirely different in mood. The snowdrop moves in the lightest breeze; it opens responsively to warmth and is eagerly visited by bees in search of early nectar. And the green of its central tube makes an essential focus.

▶ Beth Chatto has gone all-white in this area of her gravel garden, but this just serves to highlight the range of different shapes, notably of domed allium heads and the spiky ruffs of *Eryngium giganteum. The solidity of these plants is softened by the haze of flowering grass, Stipa tenuissima.*

▶▶ *The June-flowering* Ammi majus *is a favourite annual with us, which we treat as a biennial, sowing seed under cold glass in September, so as to get large plants, 1.8m/6ft or more tall. It is purest white, but with an open structure and we further break up its whiteness by interplanting with a 'blue' larkspur,* Consolida *'Blue Cloud'. This has loose, relaxed-looking spikes (45cm/30in).*

▲ White Japanese anemones – here, Anemone x hybrida 'Honorine Jobert' – contrast happily with any colour and they have their own inbuilt contrasts with a green central knob surrounded by yellow stamens. The background is Clematis rehderiana.

▼ The July-flowering regal lily, Lilium regale, has pinkish-purple-flushed buds with the flush remaining on the outside of the flower's open bloom. Its stamens are yellow. No lack of life and contrast, here. The scent is overwhelming. One bloom in a room is plenty.

candidum. The single white Japanese anemone, 'Honorine Jobert' (1m/40in or more), has a central green knob for an eye, framed by a circle of yellow lashes. From late July to mid-October, it flowers non-stop and, far from being assertive, makes a perfect background for summer bedding of any colour or mixture of colours you may fancy.

Members of the daisy tribe nearly all have a central disc of yellow florets. When these daisies have been doubled, as in certain chrysanthemums and Shasta daisies (*Leucanthemum* x *superbum*), so that they are unrelieved white, don't have too much of them, especially if, as with the Shastas and certain phloxes, their leaves are dark, heavy and solemn.

The white form of sweet rocket, *Hesperis matronalis* var. *albiflora* (1.2m/4ft), is unbrokenly white, but this can be softened by mixing it with anchusas (see 'Blue') or if it is seen in shade, especially the dappled shade of trees above it, and that is anyway where it likes to grow. White honesty or money flower, *Lunaria annua* var. *albiflora* (90cm/36in), is a similar plant but much more elegant, the white flowers on a pyramid with gaps between them. It contrasts wonderfully with the acid, greeny yellow of *Smyrnium perfoliatum*, where there is shade about.

If a rather solid white flower can be grown in shade, that will mitigate its stare. The arum lily (called calla lily in many countries), *Zantedeschia aethiopica*, from South Africa, included in 'Green' for its deep, glossy spear-shaped foliage (see pages 98 and 99), has blank white spathes, albeit relieved by the yellow central, club-shaped spadix. Each flower lasts for three weeks, unless scorched by extra-strong sunshine – which is quite probable, as it flowers in June-July – so you are making it happy by giving it shade as well as getting more enjoyment from it.

Photographing white flowers is always tricky – in sunlight, quite impossible. Either you expose for white and everything else looks dark, or you get it right for the surround, while the white is blank and featureless. In shade is my only chance, as an amateur snapshotter.

I have mentioned yellow and white as being highly compatible within the same flower. So they are on a larger scale, as between flower and leaf, and especially in spring, when much young foliage is bright greeny yellow and there is white blossom on trees and shrubs. A white and yellow border can be very effective.

As early as March, I have the handsome evergreen *Helleborus* hybrid, *H.* x *nigercors*, with trusses of large white blooms, next to a

▲ In a prominent position on Lutyens's circular steps, where it shouts 'look at me', I have planted the shrubby, grey-leaved Convolvulus cneorum, which needs the best drainage available and gets it here. Its leaves are grey. It is a basker.

▼ Single white arabis, the seed strain Snowcap, makes a pleasing carpet to early yellow tulip, the Fosteriana hybrid 'Yellow Emperor'. Both are flowering in March. White and yellow are always successful teammates.

thick clump of the *Narcissus cyclamineus* hybrid 'Jetfire', deep yellow with a light orange trumpet. Almost as early, I sometimes combine *Arabis* Snowcap, raised from seed sown the previous spring, with Fosteriana hybrid tulip, 'Yellow Purissima'. This has short stems, as befits the earliness of the season, but the blooms are large. So are its leaves. Rather than having them overlaying the arabis, you may prefer to grow them in adjacent groups, the arabis in front. Tulips like the Lily-flowered 'White Triumphator' contrast pleasingly with yellow doronicums (leopard's bane). In late summer and autumn, I like the combination I described in 'Orange': *Cosmos bipinnatus* 'Purity' (1.8m/6ft), white with a yellow disc, next to the apricot-orange dahlia, 'David Howard' (see page 46).

Shrubs with yellow leaves include *Philadelphus coronarius* 'Aureus', whose beautiful young foliage is quickly joined, in May, by white blossom, and *Physocarpus opulifolius* in one of its yellow-leaved forms, 'Dart's Gold' or 'Luteus'. The latter is worth growing entirely as a foliage shrub, the flowers being of little account. Stool it back every winter and enjoy its spring foliage, perhaps with an underplanting of the airy white narcissus, 'Thalia' or, later on, of white pheasant's eye, *Narcissus poeticus* var. *recurvus*.

White borders and, on a larger scale, white gardens will always have their advocates. The example at Sissinghurst Castle and its initiation by Vita Sackville-West continues to influence garden designers all over the world. The famous Lutyens-designed Sissinghurst bench seat will be included, perhaps reduced in size and probably painted white, unlike the original, which was never in the white garden anyway. 'And this is our little Sissinghurst,' I was told on a visit to an arboretum in North Carolina. There was

▲ A very unusual Berkheya *species from South Africa, grown in The Old Vicarage garden at East Ruston in Norfolk. This is the kind of structural plant that always catches the eye, whatever the colour of its flowers. One just hopes that it will survive the winter or, at the least, set masses of good seed.*

▶ Phlox paniculata *'Norah Leigh' should have only the narrowest green stripe along the centre of each leaf. This means that it has a fluttering, dancing look but it also has little vigour. Its pale mauve flowers are perfectly in keeping, in my opinion, though others go to the trouble of removing them. Interplanted here with the purple-flowered annual,* Browallia americana.

a central, white-painted gazebo and beds around it where white impatiens predominated. Fairly deep shade is really the only good excuse for white-painted garden furniture or accessories, like bridges or doors. Out in the open, they will seize the eye at the expense of everything else. That may be your intention; whitewashing is a covering-up act. If you must have white, make sure that the paint used is not dead white, but softened by some other colour while still giving a white impression. And make sure that you keep it clean!

The flowers in these all-white gardens are always diluted by the inclusion of grey and glaucous and white-variegated foliage, which is especially compatible with white, supportive without being competitive. Some plants, like the Californian tree poppy, *Romneya coulteri* (1.2m/4ft), combine the right colours both in their flowers (white) and foliage (glaucous, in this case). But the poppy has a mass of bright yellow stamens. I think that helps. As with the blue borders and gardens already discussed, so long as the general impression of a white garden remains white, then the introduction of compatible colours with it will improve the picture.

Thus, a white delphinium having a black central 'bee' would be every bit as good as a column of pure white. A rose species, *Rosa serafinoi*, with quite tiny white flowers but aromatic foliage, was included in the Sissinghurst white garden, near to a bench. Late in the season, it came out in a rash of small scarlet hips. I liked that.

Phlox paniculata 'Norah Leigh' is grown for the large white area, in its leaves, that surrounds a quite small central sliver of green. When it flowers, the panicle is a discreet pale mauve, perfectly in keeping, it seems to me. But purists hate this and remove the inflorescence before it can disgrace them (and the plant) – surely a wanton act of castration; the plant never again looks entirely right.

As grey- and glaucous-leaved plants need all the sun they can get in order to bring out their strongest colouring, white gardens depending on them are always in full sunshine. I remember how effective one grey-and-white garden was when approached through a deeply shaded avenue within an orchard of apple trees. This garden, out in the sun, was at the end of the avenue and gradually assumed a crescendo of importance, as light succeeded darkness. (The actual arrival was a slight disappointment, as all the beds were surrounded with wire netting against rabbits. The

◄ Globes of white agapanthus are a strong feature. They here contrast with magenta Lychnis coronaria and the stripy bamboo Pleioblastus variegatus *in front, and the annual orach,* Atriplex hortensis *var.* rubra, *behind. But if agapanthus are jostled by too much neighbourly nudging, they won't flower freely.*

▲ *Seakale,* Crambe maritima, *with domes of white, honey-scented flowers in May, has glaucous foliage. It really needs the best drainage and full exposure, so is at the front of my Long Border. Behind, is an aquilegia seed strain in a dashing contrast of purple and white. It sells well as 'Magpie', but correct killjoys prefer the unmemorable 'William Guiness' (sorry, Mr Guiness).*

► Yucca gloriosa *(up to 2m/7ft or more) flowering, in early September, in the Exotic Garden. It doesn't flower every year but usually every other if the plant is well fed. No one could say of it: 'This is too much' — or could they? The stiff leaves (see also page 163) have nasty points, which we remove where they project over a path.*

practicalities of gardening constantly thwart our best intentions.)

The importance of green in a white garden should not be overlooked, either. At Sissinghurst, there is a background of yew hedging along one side of the rectangle and one half of the garden is devoted to a formal layout of clipped box rectangles. Sometimes these become too dominant and their height is reduced.

A white border or garden is undoubtedly fun to do and it is easily humanized. White love-in-a-mist (*Nigella damascena*) (30cm/12in) never looks too solid (as dwarfened impatiens can), as the whiskery green ruff around the flower and the green centre, which will be the puffed-out seed pod, prevent that. *Omphalodes linifolia* (30cm/12in) is one of the most delightful white-flowered annuals, like a quality gypsophila and with the advantage of glaucous foliage. You can make an early March sowing under glass, bring the seedlings on in individual pots and run them through the bare areas in your white garden, in late April, to make a connecting theme. The white version of *Campanula persicifolia* is good for the same purpose, especially on the heavy soil that it enjoys. But that is a hardy perennial and will sow itself in welcome, if unexpected places at the foot of shrubs or in hedge bottoms.

The *Clematis viticella* hybrid, 'Alba Luxurians', is a vogue plant with good-taste gardeners because its swarm of flowers is not just white, but includes green in the tips of its sepals. Sometimes the entire flower is green, sometimes all white; it keeps you guessing.

Although I wouldn't limit my use of it to a white garden, the grass, *Miscanthus sinensis* 'Variegatus' (2m/7ft when established), makes a lively and graceful foliage feature throughout the summer and autumn if a single clump of it is sited, here and there, where it can rise head and shoulders above the plantings around it. It has broad bands of white either side of the green central area of each long leaf and it has a fountain-like habit.

Another good plant for our purpose is the bramble, *Rubus thibetanus* (1.5m/5ft), which has grey, pinnate leaves and even paler, prickly stems. Its branches arch a little. An essential caring task is to cut the whole plant to the ground at winter's end (its leaves are lost in autumn but the stems continue to be beautiful). Young stems are what you want. The old growth, if left, is not nearly so attractive and will flower, rather disgracingly. This shrub suckers a bit but the suckers are easily removed, at the same time as you prune.

▲ *There is lots of white love-in-a-mist in the white garden at Sissinghurst, but I even prefer it, as here in Beth Chatto's garden, with the lilac globes of* Allium cristophii *scattered through it. More punchy, wouldn't you say?*

▼ *On the ledge of a slightly raised bed, woodruff (*Galium odoratum*), which is purest white with bright green foliage, has crept into a hummock of aubrieta. It will kill the aubrieta if I let it, so (resolution!) I mustn't.*

▲ *A large-flowered clematis that is dead white all through is less satisfying than one with purple stamens, for instance, or one, as in this case – 'Huldine' – with a pale mauve, translucent underside. Give this old variety full sun and if it is then still too leafy for the amount of flower produced, move it.*

One of the great assets of white gardens and borders, yet to be discussed, is their romantic ghostliness as late evening merges into a moonlit night (where are you, moon?). You may need mosquito repellent and I hope its smell will not drown the delicious fragrance of night-flowering white plants. They are frequently tubular or trumpet-shaped and designed to attract pollinating moths, which have a long, nectar-questing proboscis.

There is no point in night-flowerers being coloured and most are naturally white, although humans have persuaded some of them to be coloured. Many do not flourish in cool-temperate climates like ours but we can grow daturas and brugmansias, either as annuals – *Datura meteloides* being one of the best for that purpose – or as tender shrubs in containers, to be brought out in the summer months.

The best *Nicotiana* for scent and for showing up at night is the straight white *N. alata* (syn. *N. affinis*). It is in a state of collapse until evening arrives and it stiffens up. Another, and handsomer as a plant, is *N. sylvestris* (1.8m/6ft). I am passionate about this plant, but unfortunately it has, of recent years, become difficult to grow well on account of the virulent downy mildew fungus which attacks it (and other nicotianas). From spring-sown seed, it generally gets into its stride in August. In sheltered positions, old plants will survive the winter for several years. This species has a splendid upright carriage and a foundation of large, bright green paddle-leaves. The long white tubular flowers open only at the mouth. They hang downwards, by day, without actually wilting, but at night lift themselves to the horizontal and exhale a strong, creamy fragrance with none of the roughness of *N. alata*. Dead blooms turn brown and remain on the plant, which is particularly noticeable when it happens on white-flowered plants. Many ladies dote on white-flowered camellias, but seem totally oblivious of their bush also being covered with brown, faded blooms, completely spoiling the picture. Frost or wind are invariably blamed for the camellias' plight, never original sin. With both camellias and this nicotiana, it is worth conducting dead flower removal sessions, although a camellia may tediously demand the services of a stepladder.

Everything has a price; the romance of white must be paid for.

Anemone x hybrida 'Honorine Jobert'
Japanese anemone
Height: 1m/3ft
Spread: 45cm/18in
Hardy, sun or partial shade
The flowers, saucers of white with a green centre and ring of yellow stamens, appear over a long period from midsummer to late autumn. They have a clear-cut quality about them and mix well with many colours and plants. Interplant colonies with vigorous bulbs, such as *Allium cristophii*.

◀ Begonia F₁ 'Stara White'
Height: 30cm/12in
Spread: 30cm/12in
Tender, sun or part shade
A fibrous-rooted begonia for summer bedding. Raise from seed sown in February at 25°C. Harden off for June planting. Will flower continuously till first frost. The fairly loose, relaxed habit is welcome, as is the copper-tinted foliage as a background to the flowers.

Crambe cordifolia
Height: 2.4m/8ft
Spread: 1.8m/6ft
Hardy, sun
This large coarse-leaved plant produces a haze of small white flowers suspended above it in early summer. Even after blooming the structure of the flowering stems is worth leaving for its airy decorative quality. Watch out for slugs. Plant bright red oriental poppies near it or clothe it with an annual climber, such as *Rhodochiton atrosanguineus*.

◀ Dianthus 'Haytor White'
Height: 30cm/12in
Spread: 40cm/16in
Hardy, light soil in sun
A perennial pink with well shaped, fully double, fragrant flowers, June to autumn. Nice for button-holes. Renew every third year from cuttings of non-flowering shoots taken any time spring to autumn.

Exochorda x macrantha 'The Bride'
Pearl bush
Height: 1.8m/6ft
Spread: 2.4m/8ft
Hardy, sun or light shade
Long arching stems are covered in pure-white flowers in the late spring. Prune back hard immediately after flowering. Plant late-flowering yellow or orange tulips with it.

Galanthus 'Atkinsii'
Snowdrop
Height: up to 25cm/10in
Spread: 5cm/2in
Hardy, light shade
One of the earliest and tallest snowdrops, with flowers like teardrops, excellent for starting new colonies. Good for highlighting dark hellebores and as sheets in shady perennial borders where hostas and rodgersias will follow.

Gypsophila paniculata 'Bristol Fairy'
Baby's breath
Height: 1.2m/4ft
Spread: 1.2m/4ft
Hardy, sun
Airy sprays of double, white flowers on wiry stems appear from mid to late summer. Its neat, unassertive blooms are useful for softening the effect of red plantings. *G. p.* 'Flamingo' is the double, pale pink form.

Helleborus x nigercors
Hellebore
Height: 30cm/12in
Spread: 45cm/18in
Hardy, light shade
A hybrid with bold leaves and a large number of flowers per stem, each a wheel of creamy white that ages to green. Early yellow narcissi make good companions.

◀ Hesperis matronalis var. albiflora
Sweet rocket
Height: 1.2m/4ft
Spread: 30cm/12in
Hardy, sun to medium shade
A short-lived perennial that is usually treated as a biennial for late spring and early summer bedding. Try it with blue-flowered *Anchusa azurea*. Good for colonizing in shade.

◄ **Hyacinthus orientalis 'Carnegie'**
Hyacinth
Height: 30cm/12in
Spread: 20cm/8in
Hardy, sun
A satisfactory mid-season hyacinth for pot, window box or garden culture. Looks good scattered fairly widely among blue or yellow pansies or violas.

▲ *Impatiens tinctoria*
Busy Lizzie
Height: 2m/7ft
Spread: 1.5m/5ft
Slightly tender, part shade
Tuberous-rooted perennial for good, moist soil; generally housed after the first frost, but can be overwintered in the ground if covered with protective litter. Flowers from June. Protect young growth against capsid bugs.

Lunaria annua var. albiflora
White-flowered honesty
Height: 90cm/36in
Spread: 30cm/12in
Hardy, sun or light shade
Glistening white flowers in late spring cheer up shady corners, where this biennial can be mixed with the acid, greeny yellow of *Smyrnium perfoliatum*. *L.a.* 'Alba Variegata' has similar flowers but also splashes of white on the foliage.

Magnolia stellata ►
Height: 2m/7ft
Spread: 2.4m/8ft
Hardy, sun, neutral or acid soil
Early spring-flowering magnolia, very prolific from an early age. The buds are usually flushed pink. Good spread of blossom; so, if frosted while flowering, a new crop will soon replace the old.

◄ *Narcissus poeticus var. recurvus*
Pheasant's eye
Height: 45cm/18in
Spread: 15cm/6in
Hardy, sun or light shade
One of the whitest narcissus, shallow cups rimmed with red, and also one of the latest flowering, in May. It has the best fragrance of all. The double form flowers two weeks later. *N.* 'Thalia', with abundant flowers, is earlier.

Nicotiana sylvestris
Height: 1.8m/6ft
Spread: 60cm/24in
Fairly hardy, sun or partial shade
A tall perennial usually treated as a biennial or annual, with large sticky leaves and large heads of white flowers with very long tubes that look like fireworks going off. They are very fragrant at night. Particularly useful at the back of borders.

Omphalodes linifolia
Venus' navelwort
Height: 30cm/12in
Spread: 15cm/6in
Hardy, sun
White forget-me-not-type flowers over glaucous foliage appear from late spring throughout the summer, depending on time of sowing. It is a useful annual for filling gaps, especially in a white garden, and will self-sow on light soils.

Philadelphus coronarius **'Aureus'**
Mock orange
Height: 2.4m/8ft
Spread: 1.5m/5ft
Hardy, light shade
A shrub with lime-green to greenish-yellow foliage and masses of fragrant white flowers in early summer. It needs to be planted in dappled shade to prevent the foliage scorching, but with enough sun to bring out the leaf colouring. Prune back flowering shoots after the blossom fades.

Phlox paniculata **'Norah Leigh'**
Height: 1m/40in
Spread: 45cm/18in
Hardy, sun to light shade
One of the whitest-leaved perennial plants, the whole leaf, apart from a small area of green in the centre, covered in white. Can be used in areas of the border where long-term white is required. The flowers are pale mauve, darker in the centre.

Romneya coulteri
Californian tree poppy
Height: 1.2m/4ft
Spread: 2m/7ft
Hardy, sun
A delightful crinkly poppy flower of pure white with a large central yellow boss of stamens. The flowers appear throughout the summer and are well set off by the blue-green foliage, which by itself can be rather scruffy. Cut right down in winter and interplant colonies with spring-flowering bulbs.

Sanguisorba tenuifolia **'Alba'**
Burnet
Height: 90cm/36in
Spread: 45cm/18in
Hardy, sun or partial shade
Arching stems topped with fluffy dangles of white blossom. The foliage has a delicate quality that is worth being able to see. For contrast, underplant with *Papaver commutatum* 'Ladybird', or associate with *Crocosmia* 'Lucifer'.

Cheerful YELLOW

We have at last arrived at cheerful, stimulating yellow. The colour of sunlight, it lifts the spirits. Yellow is highly visible, which makes many people nervous of wearing it.

There is a snob element about yellow, too. In part this has to do with the word itself, which does not fall agreeably on the ear. The German *gelb* is no better; it barks (French is luckier with the forward sound of *jaune*). In both English and German we will, whenever possible, substitute gold or golden (*goldner*), which additionally provides its own atmosphere of riches, comfort and well being. Gold is, in fact, a rather sulky-coloured metal (with none of the sparkle of silver) and the fact that very few flowers come in reality near to gold is just as well.

Yellow in gardens is the people's colour. 'All those yellow daisies' will be the sneering comment of self-appointed arbiters of good taste. But it should be an emotional colour, lifting to the spirits. 'The sun always shines from a yellow planting', wrote Nori and Sandra Pope in their book on colour. A bed of yellow rudbeckias ('Indian Summer' is the one I most fancy) towards sunset is transfixing, even when the sky is overcast.

This warmth of light predominates in autumn, but the sharpness of spring also suits yellow and it goes particularly well with spring green. Which is the reason for our seeing so many yellow daffodils growing in grass. The little hoop-petticoat daffodil in its primrose yellow form, *Narcissus bulbocodium* var. *citrinus*, is a winner. Never did a daffodil dance like this. Start it in a piece of undernourished turf (mine is beneath an oak) and it will do the

◄ *Among the softest of primrose yellows in early spring are the flowers, borne on still naked branches of* Corylopsis. *This is* C. glabrescens *and it is sweetly lemon-scented on the air. Belonging to the Hamamelis family, it does not like alkaline soil, but is otherwise easy and lovely to pick for the house.*

▲ One of the earliest daffodils in flower and coinciding with the late Dutch crocuses, is our native Lent lily, Narcissus pseudonarcissus. *Given a start by my mother, who used to raise batches from seed and then plant them out, they now self-sow freely, looking better on their own or with other small species, than with large, man-made chaps.*

▼ The winter aconite, Eranthis hyemalis, *is vastly cheering on its first appearing, in January. It goes well with the mauve Crocus tommasinianus.*

▶ The emerging shoots of herbaceous peonies, in early spring, are usually some lively shade of carmine, which should be taken advantage of by interplanting some early flowerer like the primroses, here. Contrasting hyacinths also make good partners and so does the little faintly blue-tinted, white-flowered bulb, Ipheion uniflorum.

rest for you, seeding itself till you have drifts of it by the hundred.

Before the daffodils we have had winter aconites (*Eranthis hyemalis*) and Dutch yellow crocuses. And we should not be snobby about the flowers of dandelions, which open to early spring sunshine and enliven countryside road verges. Enamelled celandines are responsive in the same way; it is hard not to compare them with crowds of smiling children's faces. Odd that, in the gardening world, dandelions are widely disapproved of whereas celandines, offering a great many different manifestations, are quite a cult. 'Brazen Hussy', has the usual vivid yellow celandine flowers, but such deep purple leaves that I include it in 'Black' (page 187). But if you let celandines loose in your borders, their tiny tubers will quickly get spread around and become quite a plague, each spring. So long as you are aware of this danger, it can be kept under control.

Primroses, which belong no less to spring, are quite another type of yellow, their softness giving rise to the designation primrose yellow, which is often applied to other flowers, such as the lemony-scented *Corylopsis glabrescens* with dangles of pale yellow blossom, nice to pick. Even those gardeners (and they are numerous) who dislike most yellow flowers have to make an exception of yellows such as these and they (we, for I include myself as a primrose yellow lover) are always on the lookout for

▲ Iris pseudacorus 'Variegata' is one of the most scintillatingly fresh variegated plants in the spring garden. Later, the variegation melts away, but it will return the following spring.

▼ This elder, Sambucus racemosa 'Plumosa Aurea', is grown entirely for its foliage. Hard pruning each winter gives rise to the handsomest leaves – copper when young, lime-green later – and prevents flowering, which is no loss. Over-exposure results in summer scorch; too much shade, in wan colouring. Strike a happy medium (not to be confused with Epimedium).

flowers of that shade, which is so amenable to being combined with other colours, even pink.

Before you next decry fields of rape in their May flowering season, consider whether their patchwork over the otherwise green spring countryside is not really a joyful addition. The shade of yellow includes quite a dose of alleviating green. They fill the air with a sweet honey scent. (Later, admittedly, a cabbagey smell is liable to take over.) I think it is because a new system of grants made the growing of rape profitable, that its sudden appearance in a countryside where we were not familiar with its presence went counter to our natural conservatism.

One of the more clamorous flowering shrubs of spring is *Kerria japonica* in its double form 'Pleniflora'. Along its bright green young stems (which can achieve 3m/10ft against a wall) are arranged strings of very fully double pompons. This can be quite a scruffy shrub as, to look smart, it needs regular pruning by the removal of flowered wands and the encouragement (by feeding) of new ones. Well grown, its ebullience is infectious. But, in better taste (I write in the language of the good taste fellowship) is the single-flowered type plant, whose colouring seems to be softer. In fact, it is not, but the shadows included within the double kerria bloom make it seem a darker colour. Only recently have I seen (and bought) a single kerria called 'Albescens', which really is pale yellow and, I have to say, charming in its own way. No doubt it will go far to assuage the doubts and fears of bright yellow haters.

Among the most intense and vibrant yellow flowers of spring is the kingcup, *Caltha palustris* (30cm/12in), a clumpy plant which, in the wild, inhabits dyke sides and many other boggy places. In a garden setting we justifiably intensify its impact even further with the tightly doubled 'Flore Pleno'. I have been most struck by it in the wild on the Outer Hebridean island of Lewis, which is on the whole, in its large central area, of a depressing drabness. Yet, where there is a bog (and there are many bogs), the kingcups are there by the acre in breathtaking abundance.

A few weeks later, and in the same conditions, they are followed by the wild flag iris, *Iris pseudacorus* (90cm/36in), which is scarcely less lively. Around a garden pond (alongside its natural partner, the water dropwort, *Oenanthe crocata*), it may be rather too aggressive but our civilizing influence can be seen at work here, too. Var. *bastardii* (who he? and why are bastards always assumed to be male?) is decorous pale yellow with thin, dark veining, while 'Variegata', much weaker growing, has wonderfully

▲ In its modest way, Spiraea thunbergii *is a delight in latest autumn – early winter, really – when its foliage changes colour before falling. It has a long flowering season in early spring and can be pruned after that.*

▼ Spotted laurels need to be really heavily spotted and proud of their spots if they are to be effective, as is Aucuba japonica 'Crotonifolia'. The leaf shape is strong, which makes the necessary contrast with a diffuse surface pattern.

fresh yellow variegation of its young spring foliage.

Yellow is the colour most easily produced by a plant, next to green. Many plants, like this iris, are yellow at their first appearance in spring, changing to green later. In autumn, it is the other way about; green is withdrawn, leaving clear yellow before leaf fall, as becomes so luminously apparent in trees like the maidenhair tree, *Ginkgo biloba*, the tulip tree, *Liriodendron tulipifera*, or our own field maple, *Acer campestre*. Often seeing this out of the corner of my eye (my mind a little absent), I think it is a wild broom (*Cytisus scoparius*) in flower. It is easy to become disorientated. The golden yellow fruit of some pyracanthas in autumn catches me unawares thinking it is the deep crocus-yellow *Berberis* x *stenophylla*.

Yellow in young foliage has a strong attraction, but can take on a hectic, feverish tone when the sun is hot and the plant is dry at the root. This, you may be sure, will be followed by burning. The affected foliage will die in patches and turn a most unsavoury brown. A little overhead shade will help to prevent this condition from developing (too much shade and you lose the yellow altogether), as also will a heavy drenching of the roots in anticipation of possible danger ahead. Again, the yellowish foliage on young and vigorous shrub shoots is often less inclined to burn than the foliage on older, flowered growth. An example is *Philadelphus coronarius* 'Aureus', the popular, yellow-leaved version of our European mock orange and already described in 'White' for its beautiful foliage and blossom (swooningly fragrant). You could prune this entirely for foliage effect, heading all its previous season's growth back to a stool. Or, less severely, you could quickly follow its May flowering with a strict pruning out of all the flowered branches.

I am very fond of my heavily yellow-spotted laurel, *Aucuba japonica* 'Crotonifolia' (though this kind of undisciplined variegation is widely detested), but have to admit that it goes through a bad period in early summer, when a quite high proportion of its leaves scorch to brown in patches. This happened less before the shade from a nearby mulberry disappeared following the big storm of October 1987. But my bush is healthy, by and large, and I am prepared to pick off its worst leaves by hand. It is an evergreen, and the trouble is not of long duration. Nearby, I have an ash called *Fraxinus pennsylvanica* 'Aucubifolia'! This has yellow-variegated leaves splashed haphazardly. I love it but seem to have not a single friend who

▲ *Yellow and orange combine excitingly in this spring scene of wallflowers, 'Queen of Sheba' Lily-flowered tulips and* Arum creticum *(on the right). The bright yellow arum flowers, in which the spathe makes a spiral near the tip, may not last longer than a few days, but what exciting days!*

▶ *An early August scene of luxuriant enjoyment in the Exotic Garden. The pungently yellow corn marigold,* Chrysanthemum segetum, *lifts your spirits. It contrasts with mauve* Verbena bonariensis *and both are self-sowers. Cannas, dahlias and a young Japanese banana behind.*

can share the pleasure it gives me. Someone must surely turn up, some day. It is so beautiful in spring that Fergus says he won't look at it in case he changes his mind. The prototype, which first inspired me, was in Holland Park, west London. I do hope it is still standing.

Sometimes luminous yellow is a bit too much even for me. I am thinking of the version of false acacia, *Robinia pseudoacacia*, called 'Frisia'. There is quite a vogue for it, but this can easily be overdone and look self-conscious in the 'look-at-me' show-off manner of a spoilt child. In certain suburbs, it is in every other front garden. Far from losing intensity of colouring as the season wears on, it becomes even more insistent in autumn. However, let us be fair (how boring). The pinnate leaf is a pretty shape. Part of our dislike is because this tree is so often juxtaposed in obvious contrast with a purple beech or Norway maple. And part is simply with becoming sated by repetition, which is not the tree's fault. The example I have most admired was just one of the robinia among many grey-leaved, light-catching white willows, *Salix alba*.

A little touch of bright yellow is often all that is needed for effect. Thus in a bedding scheme of wallflowers, I sometimes like to combine the most startling and pure yellow 'Cloth of Gold' with deep purple 'Ruby Gem'. But only one plant of the yellow is needed to three of the purple (this is the same story as when bedding with white).

A favourite annual with Fergus and me is the corn marigold, *Chrysanthemum segetum* (60cm/24in), or *Xanthophthalmum segetum*, to give it its horrid new name, which has simple yellow daisies as bright, both rays and disc, as they come. We allow it to self-sow in our rather sophisticated exotic garden, where there are many startling foliage plants, like bananas and palms, as well as cannas and dahlias. The marigold's is often the only yellow present. Its leaves are grey-green, the flowers numerous but scattered as in a constellation. The plant is irrepressibly cheerful. It makes you smile.

The yellow daisies like smaller, taller and rather less dazzling versions of dandelions, which naturally inhabit a permanent meadow's flora in summer, compose an important element in the overall tapestry. These are the hawkweeds (*Hieracium*), hawk's-beards (*Crepis*), hawkbits (*Leontodon*) and goat's beards (*Tragopogon*). They are difficult to distinguish and a headache to the systematic botanists, yet all have an individuality of habit and shading which distinguishes them when seen in a meadow

▲ Since I have allowed
our topiary lawn to
become an uncut meadow
during the summer
months, it has filled up
with self-appointed wild
flowers, notably buttercups
and hawksbeards, which
are yellow and at their
jolliest in the late morning.
The Lutyens-designed seat,
known as the family pew
(my father used to
photograph the assembled
family on it), is in the
background.

◄◄ By no means all of
the red-hot pokers are in
brash shades of orange.
The rather late-flowering
Kniphofia 'Torchbearer'
(1.5m/5ft) has a lot of
green in its yellow
colouring. Its concentrated
flowering season is fairly
short but worth waiting
for.

setting. Their abundance is amazing. When I stopped mowing
and weed-killing a considerable area of lawn in my garden, these
yellow daisies moved in at speed, jollying up the scene from mid-
May till late summer. They are temperamental, remaining closed
till well into the morning, opening wide only in sunshine and
closing again, however sunny, quite early in the afternoon. And
they follow the sun, which should always be behind you when you
are looking at a sea of yellow daisies. How could one fail to
respond to them? Throw in some white moon daisies, some red
and some white clover and, of course, a range of yellow buttercups
and nothing more is needed. As a child, I loved to shuffle my feet
through a field of buttercups so that my shoes became yellow with
their pollen.

Blue with yellow always makes for a happy contrast. In August,
some years more than others, we have a hatch in our meadows of
the Common Blue butterfly and it likes to feed on the yellow
daisies of the autumnal hawkbit, *Leontodon autumnalis*. Yellow
daisies assume increasing importance in my borders as the
summer progresses and assumes the warmth of light that belongs
to autumn. Sunflowers, coneflowers and senecios are among the
most dominant. There is a perennial sunflower that is a particular
favourite of mine, *Helianthus* 'Monarch' (2-2.4m/7-8ft). It repays
being grown well, frequently dividing and replanting its tuberous

A splendid meadow effect is gained, in July, by widely spaced clumps of the tall yellow daisy, Inula magnifica (1.8m/6ft). The grass around them is cut shortly before they flower, but is full of pheasant's-eye narcissus in spring. We boost the inulas by mulching them in winter.

The Inula magnifica's 15cm/6in daisies have very long rays, which shiver in a breeze.

roots in improved soil, in spring. Then, as its inflorescence starts to branch, I disbud some stems (only some) so that all the energy is concentrated in the terminal bud. The flowers will then be really large (more than 15cm/6in across), with several rows of rich yellow rays surrounding a black disc. This never looks better than when seen against a blue sky.

Another flower that is thrilling to see in this way, is *Mahonia x media* 'Lionel Fortescue' (2.4m/8ft). It is an evergreen shrub with pinnate leaves and a stiffly upright habit. It flowers in November. Every rosette of leaves explodes at the centre into an upright bouquet of yellow flowers arranged along stiff, yet thread-like racemes. If the weather is right, honey bees, late on the wing, love to visit and all this should be admired against a blue sky. It surprisingly often happens.

Not all yellows are invigorating. That of many hypericums – the St John's worts – tends to be heavy and lustreless. I am thinking in particular of the widely grown, long-flowering and thoroughly obliging shrubby 'Hidcote' (1.2m/4ft). You can and should prune it all hard back each winter. I often see it in a front garden with pink hydrangeas. This does not work. Sometimes a red rose is of the company. That doesn't work either. Another, though less hardy, shrubby hypericum, 'Rowallane' (1.5m/5ft), with rather more deeply cupped blooms and a gloss on its petals,

is far more agreeable beneath the rose, combined with pink *Anemone hupehensis* 'Bowles' Pink'. It looks its best in Ireland, where it originated.

I will conclude with some of the yellow flowers that give me most pleasure. There is the chrome yellow, crocus-like *Sternbergia lutea*, which starts its growing season by flowering in autumn. It needs lots of baking sunshine but even in England, on chalky soils in Kent, I have admired it in sheets.

I have already mentioned the early-flowering Fosteriana hybrid tulip, 'Yellow Purissima', combined with *Arabis* Snowcap. It has large, beautifully shaped blooms above correspondingly large leaves with a bluish cast to them. The colouring is soft yet bright, touched with green. It looks almost too fragile for the season, but the occasions when we are lucky with the weather are memorable and threat of danger intensifies our pleasure.

Spartium junceum (2m/7ft), the Spanish broom, is incredibly bright and luminous but without the coarse heartiness that we

often associate with brooms. Its colouring is fresher, the flowers are larger. The shrub's habit is clumsy. Its hollow, rush-like shoots should be upright, but great chunks of a bush will be blown sideways. If you have the space and sufficiently relaxed surroundings to be able to allow this, it has an endearing charm. If not, you can prune heavily each early spring and terminal flower spikes will be borne on the young shoots. Delicious, airborne scent, transporting you to its Mediterranean habitats. It loves the sea.

There are a tremendous number of species and hybrid mulleins, but the noblest, in Fergus's and my estimation is the biennial *Verbascum olympicum* (2m/7ft). In its second year, a stout, upright stem branches obliquely into a symmetrical candelabrum of clear yellow blossom. Splendid against a dark background. It can be grouped or treated as solo incidents, either at the back of a border or in its centre or at the front.

Hunnemannia fumariifolia (30cm/12in), the tulip poppy, is an annual or short-lived perennial related to *Eschscholzia*. One of its great attractions are the glaucous, fingered leaves. Above these hover bowl-shaped poppy flowers of a strong yet kindly yellow. Alas, this is not too easily grown well in our climate, but it can be done. It hates disturbance but once settled in will give a mouth-watering display in late summer and autumn, looking good with purple *Verbena rigida* or with an apron of blue *Anagallis linifolia*.

Nymphaea 'Texas Dawn' might not stand out in a crowd of tropical waterlilies but certainly does in our climate. It has large, pale yellow flowers (each lasting for three days), their petals rather pointed and the blooms stand several inches above the water. It appears to be perfectly hardy and contrasts dramatically with our normal run of nymphaeas.

Tender in our climate, alas, although quite possibly hardy on the Cornish and Devon coasts, is the shrub best known as *Cassia corymbosa*, correctly *Senna corymbosa*. It is a legume of scrambling habit and, if it can survive the winter, will hoist itself among other shrubs (against a sunny wall) to 3.5m/12ft, with clusters of open pea flowers in the richest shade of butter yellow imaginable. Glossy, rich green pinnate foliage is the greatest asset. You can treat this as a tender bedding plant.

Try not to dismiss yellow as beneath your notice. It is hugely invigorating. And, combined with clear pink, the subject of the next chapter, yellow can jolt us out of habits that have become over-predictable.

Arum creticum
Height: 30cm/12in
Spread: 30cm/12in
Near-hardy (winter foliage sometimes frosted), part shade
In good moist soil, this arum grows autumn to spring; flowers mid-spring, then is dormant all summer and can be interplanted with bedding begonias or dwarf nasturtiums. Tuberous roots produce offsets and can be replanted or increased after flowering. Exciting strong yellow colouring in the most widely cultivated forms.

Caltha palustris 'Flore Pleno'
Kingcup
Height: 30cm/12in
Spread: 45cm/18in
Hardy, sun or partial shade
Produces shafts of sunlight on grey spring days with its golden, cup-shaped flowers. The single flowers have simplicity but the double 'Flore Pleno' seems to produce a more intense yellow. Good for planting in boggy soil at the edge of a pond, surrounded by greenery and reflecting water.

Centaurea glastifolia
Height: 80cm/32in
Spread: 80cm/32in
Hardy, sun
Summer-flowering perennial for a sunny border. Soft colouring and graceful habit. Any soil. *C. macrocephala* is similar and more widely grown. Larger flower heads on less branching plants. Altogether stiffer and coarser but handsome.
▶

Chrysanthemum (syn. *Xanthophthalmum*) segetum
Corn marigold
Height: 60cm/24in
Spread: 30cm/12in
Hardy, sun
An annual with fresh-looking yellow daisy flowers. It looks well with blue cornflowers, as well as mixed with hotter exotics. It is often found in wild-flower mixtures but must be sown in cultivated rather than 'meadow' situations. When happy it will self-sow.

Corylopsis glabrescens
Height: 4m/13ft
Spread: 4m/13ft
Hardy, light shade
Spring-flowering shrub on which the loose clusters of flowers appear before the leaves. It can be used in isolation or associated with something bold such as red-flowered *Rhododendron thomsonii*, which also needs acid soil.

Crocus x luteus 'Dutch Yellow'
Height: 10cm/4in
Spread: 5cm/2in
Hardy, sun or partial shade
One of the larger crocuses with big goblets of golden yellow flowers, among the first to open. It forms large clumps and is useful for placing in odd and unexpected corners as well as for filling gaps between plants yet to appear. Does not self-sow.

Eranthis hyemalis
Winter aconite
Height: 8cm/3in
Spread: 5cm/2in
Hardy, light shade
Flowers like cups of gold supported by a ruff of green leaves push up through the soil in mid to late winter. Good for planting under trees or shrubs if the soil is moist enough, or among colonies of hostas, where it will form drifts.

Erysimum cheiri 'Cloth of Gold'
Wallflower
Height: 38cm/15in
Spread: 30cm/12in
Hardy, sun
A perennial but best grown from seed each year as a biennial. Large, fragrant flowers make startling contrast with deep purple wallflower 'Ruby Gem' or use it more conventionally by combining it with hot (orange-) reds.

Helianthus 'Monarch'
Sunflower
Height: 2.4m/8ft
Spread: 1.2m/4ft
Hardy, sun
A tall perennial sunflower, with yellow ray petals and a black central disc, stately enough for the back of a border. *H.* 'Lemon Queen' is a somewhat shorter (1.8m/6ft) spreading perennial with smaller, pale yellow flowers (up to 12cm/5in across), but there are a lot of them. Good planted behind pink Japanese anemones or the pink-flowered *Persicaria amplexicaulis* 'Rosea'.

Hunnemannia fumariifolia
Tulip poppy
Height: 30cm/12in
Spread: 25cm/10in
Hardy, sun
Yellow, cup-shaped flowers carried above finely cut, glaucous foliage. It needs a warm spot and winter protection to survive and grow well. Plant with purple *Verbena rigida* or with intense blue *Anagallis linifolia*.

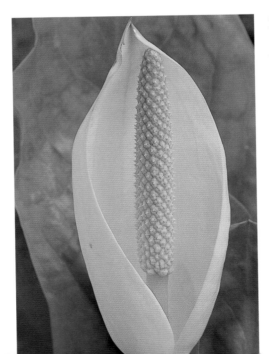

Lysichiton americanus
Yellow skunk cabbage
Height: 50cm/20in at flowering, 1m/40in later
Spread: 50cm/20in at flowering, 3m/10ft later
Hardy, sun or shade
Early spring-flowering member of the arum family for wet, marshy places. Makes a splendid colony in time, by self-sowing. Seeds carried to new areas by water. Flowers before leaves, which become large and lush.
◀

◄ *Mahonia lomariifolia*
Height: 3m/10ft
Spread: 1.8m/6ft
Hardy, partial shade
A pinnate evergreen which, in early winter, throws up long stiff spikes of yellow flowers, popular with bees. Looks good with a vigorous clematis, such as *C. x triternata* 'Rubromarginata', scrambling through it. A hard spring pruning prevents legginess. Plant where the flowers can be seen against a blue sky.

Narcissus bulbocodium* var. *citrinus
Hoop-petticoat daffodil
Height: 10cm/4in
Hardy, sun or light shade
Pale yellow lampshade flowers. It thrives and self sows in undernourished turf. Early narcissus for the border, where their dying leaves are soon concealed by neighbours, include 'February Gold', and 'March Sunshine'.

Oenothera glaziouana
Evening primrose
Height: 2m/7ft
Spread: 80cm/32in
Hardy, sun
Tallest and largest-flowered of the hardy evening primroses. Any soil. Open site. Biennial, flowering all summer in its second year. Self sows freely and often colonizes sand dunes and waste places. Flowers open at dusk but often last well into the forenoon next day, especially under overcast skies. Good theme plant in the garden but numbers must be controlled. ▼

◄ *Rudbeckia hirta* 'Indian Summer'
Black-eyed Susan
Height: 1.2m/4ft
Spread: 30cm/12in
Hardy, sun
A hybrid, with strong yellow ray petals and a black central cone, treated like an annual and sown from seed every year. Plant for early autumn with *Verbena* 'La France' in front and white Japanese anemones behind. *R. fulgida* var. *sullivantii* 'Goldsturm' is the showiest of the shorter (45cm/18in), bushier kinds.

Sinacalia tangutica
Height: 2m/7ft
Spread: indefinite
Hardy, sun or shade
A vigorous perennial for rich, moist soil. Overwinters by fleshy tubers and makes a colony with these. Pyramids of spidery flowers, late summer, above handsomely cut foliage. Looks good with *Aconitum carmichaelii* cultivars like 'Kelmscott' and with white *Hydrangea paniculata* 'Tardiva'. Fluffy seed heads in autumn, also effective. ▼

Spartium junceum
Spanish broom
Height: 2m/7ft
Spread: 2m/7ft
Hardy, sun
A stiff, upright shrub with hollow, rush-like stems, bearing quite large bright yellow scented flowers in the summer. It mixes well with pinks, such as *Lavatera* 'Bredon Springs'.

Sternbergia lutea
Height: 15cm/6in
Spread: 8cm/3in
Hardy, sun
A bright yellow goblet, very much like a crocus, appears in autumn, often late autumn, set off against strap-like leaves of dark, shiny green. It needs well-drained soil, a warm position and plenty of sun.

***Tulipa* 'Yellow Purissima'**
Height: 35cm/14in
Spread: 15cm/6in
Hardy, sun
A Fosteriana type tulip, yellow with a hint of green and large leaves, slightly glaucous.

Verbascum olympicum
Mullein
Height: 2m/7ft
Spread: 1.2m/4ft
Hardy, sun
A tall branching biennial with large spikes of yellow flowers in high summer that form a candelabrum. It can be used in groups or scattered throughout a border to add height and interest. It will self-sow, often in the most appropriate places, as does shorter *V. chaixii* which is typically yellow with purple stamens.

The Truth about PINK

Pink is the most feminine colour. Blue for a boy, pink for a girl. We all have a feminine element and most of us respond to pink flowers, if they are the 'right' shade of pink, as being harmonious and reassuring.

◄ *The single-flowered pink Japanese anemone, here* Anemone hupehensis *'Hadspen Abundance' (1.8m/3ft), has a lot to be said about it. There are usually six (here five) petals, in two ranks of three, the outer three often a deeper shade than the inner, which is interesting. The petals are broad; in a double flower, this breadth is sacrificed in favour of a large number of narrow petals; simplicity for fuss. The shade of pink is directed towards mauve and it is contrasted with yellow stamens and a green central knob. I think this works pretty well; do you? If so, try combining pink anemones with, say, yellow sunflower,* Helianthus *'Lemon Queen'.*

Not everyone. I had a friend who would on no account allow pink in her garden. In some ways, she was quite a masculine lady. Living in London, I was keen that she should meet another of my London gardening friends and she volunteered to ring him and suggest a meeting. On the phone she introduced herself by saying: 'I am a woman friend of Christopher Lloyd.' She spoke rather deliberately and paused between the words woman and friend, and her voice was so deep that Alan, at the other end of the line, wondered during the pause just what he was listening to. I will add that they got on famously.

Pink can be quite tricky – at least I find it so. It tends to veer in one of two directions. If towards red, the result is salmon; I have a problem with many salmony-coloured flowers. If towards blue, we may be in for quite an aggressive tone. I am not saying it cannot be accommodated, but it needs careful handling.

Remember 'The Queen Elizabeth' rose and the huge popularity it enjoyed in its earlier years. I had a bush (one) of it myself and, at a distance of fifty yards, seen from the kitchen window and with dark yew topiary behind, it was quite striking in a declamatory sort of way. But how sick one became of it in everyone's front garden. It is virtually impossible to integrate with any mixed planting, its own habit being stiffly upright and entirely ungraceful before you start to take notice of the bullying

abrasiveness of the flowers themselves.

Much more recently, we have 'The McCartney Rose', often miscalled 'Paul McCartney' but named in homage to him and his late wife, Linda. That is more of a Hybrid Tea than a Floribunda and its full flowers are well shaped, though still quite a shouting pink. They are, however, wonderfully scented and, while keeping my bush close to a path so that I can easily draw a bloom towards me to sniff, I have also managed to integrate this large, stiff and muscular shrub sufficiently with its surroundings of equally tall plants, for it not to stand out blatantly. It suffers, as with so many flowers in which flower size has been a major consideration in the course of breeding, from also having very large, coarse leaves and very thick stems.

Yet there are pink roses of a soft, clear colouring and having a far more accommodating habit. Of the old-fashioned kinds, there is 'Céleste', a once-flowering rose derived from *Rosa x alba*. The bush is lax in habit and has a mild tendency to sucker, so you can give presents of it to friends (it should, of course, be grown on its own roots, not grafted). The loosely doubled flowers are prettily shaped.

The modern Polyantha rose 'The Fairy' has many assets and no faults that I can think of. It is easily grown on its own roots, so I shouldn't recommend grafted plants. The neat foliage is bright green. The trusses of neatly doubled flowers, open from early July – a little later than most roses – and have a long season. The colour is pure pink and the plant is a great mixer, for use near to the margin of a mixed border. With mine I have the self-sowing Chinese chives, *Allium tuberosum* (45cm/18in), with domed heads of whitish flowers in late summer. In a Norfolk garden, I have admired a bed of it intermingled with mauve *Viola cornuta*, which has the weaving habit of many pansies and violas.

'Ballerina', a Polyantha of considerable vigour, has large panicles of single flowers in a decent, if not outstanding, shade of pink. Grafted on a strong stock, it may be inconveniently vigorous. Again I recommend plants on their own roots and the size of the shrub can be controlled by pruning.

Now for some other pink flowers of a clear, unadulterated colouring. Pinks (*Dianthus*) themselves are extremely variable, some tinged with mauve, others salmony, as in the detestable but ever-popular 'Doris'. Plants quickly become woody and need frequent replacement with young stock. Generally their owners hang on to the old ones. The desirability of renewal applies to

▲ *A soft, pure pink, untainted by mauve, is not all that common but to be treasured, as in this perennial* Sidalcea *'Elsie Heugh', with frilly margins to its petals.*

▼ *Man's aim, in developing a rotate flower, has generally been to provide it with broad, overlapping petals. But the very gappiness in the notched petals of* Lavatera cachemiriana, *a shrubby mallow, has its own relaxed charm.*

many pinks. An old-fashioned single, 'Inchmery', albeit once-flowering, is a delightful shade of clear pink and excellently scented. Furthermore, its flower colouring contrasts ideally with its glaucous-grey leaves.

Sidalceas are hardy, summer-flowering perennials with spikes of open-funnel flowers (they are obvious mallow relatives) in some shade of pink – more often than not, a difficult shade, bright and brash with a strong dash of blue in it. Some, however, are soft and pure and I would especially recommend 'Elsie Heugh' (75cm/30in). Equally well coloured is 'Sussex Beauty' (1.2m/4ft) but that needs secure support. They associate well with the old-fashioned roses that peak in June-July and with frothy pink flowers, which I'll come to later.

Mallow pink is a bright shade with a good dash of blue in it, therefore fairly uncompromising. *Lavatera* are shrubby mallows, the most popular for many years being the fast-growing, summer- and autumn-flowering *L.* 'Rosea' (2m/7ft), which is bright mallow pinky-mauve. A well-grown specimen – and it grows extremely fast – is a splendid sight in July and stares out at you over many a front garden fence. But when the very soft, pale pink (with a darker eye) sport named 'Barnsley' appeared, that largely took over in popularity. 'Blushing Bride' is even paler. Both have a tendency to throw back to straight 'Rosea'.

Most of the dandelion tribe are yellow, but *Crepis incana* (30cm/12in) is exceptional. Its toothed, greyish leaves, seen before flowering, make people say that in their garden they would weed it out. But when a soft, loose cushion of double pink flowers appears, in late June, they sing a different tune. Again, the greyish foliage makes a helpful background.

Penstemon 'Evelyn' (60cm/24in) is a pretty hardy, front-of-border plant that will survive for several years, though it benefits from a hard cut-back in spring. The leaves are fine and linear; the racemes of narrow bells, elegant and a clear enough shade of pink, with only a hint of mauve.

Hyacinths of the early-flowering florists' types, come in a range of pinks, not always distinguished in their catalogue descriptions. 'Jan Bos' is generally described as red, though actually in a particularly harsh and difficult shade of deep, bluish pink. The old 'Lady Derby' is soft and clear, but the one I should choose for general purposes, both indoors and in the garden, is 'Anna Marie'. For striking contrast, try it beneath the canopy of the young bronzy foliage of *Spiraea japonica* 'Goldflame', pruned

▲ The Lily-flowered tulip 'China Pink' is, in my view, the best in this colour. Here planted at the back of a deep, one-sided border with tall contents, it is nevertheless perfectly visible in May, enlivening the early part of the season.

▼ A pale pink hyacinth of kindly colouring but strongly shaped, with lime-green Euphorbia myrsinites in front and Erysimum 'Bowles' Mauve' behind. An April scene in Beth Chatto's garden.

in July immediately after flowering.

When it comes to choosing tulips, I generally find myself veering towards those with orange, red or yellow flowers, but one that I repeatedly return to is 'China Pink'. It is a winner, although I find it hard to explain exactly why. It is Lily-flowered, mid-season and a strong shade of impure pink with an element of blue in it. Lovely above a carpet of pink pomponette daisies (*Bellis*). But good in many contexts other than bright green lawn. Those two do not marry at all well.

I don't grow many pink dahlias, but the pink blooms of 'Pearl of Heemstede' (1.2m/4ft) have a soothing air and go well with the purple flowered *Solanum rantonnetii* and the purple-leaved *Ricinus communis* 'Carmencita'.

Pink flowers cleverly derived from a species that is normally yellow, orange or red, are rarely true pink but retain a dash of original sin. Pink oriental poppies (*Papaver orientale*) for instance, find it hard altogether to forget their scarlet origins. Nevertheless, in the neat, saucer-shaped pink 'Karine' (75cm/30in), for instance, we have a beautiful flower, while the large, frilly, frou-frou 'Juliane' is a sophisticated Miss.

Hemerocallis is naturally yellow, sometimes tawny. To have

▲ *Clear pinks, untainted by mauve or yellow, are the most satisfactory, though not all that common. You find it here in* Hebe *'Watson's Pink', over which I have grown the 'blue' clematis 'Prince Charles'. The hebe's second flowering in autumn is sometimes on the light side.*

◄◄ *In my Exotic Garden, most of the dahlias are yellow, orange or red, but I make an exception of this beautifully shaped waterlily dahlia, 'Pearl of Heemstede', which is clear, unadulterated pink. It goes well with deep mauve* Verbena bonariensis *and purple* Solanum rantonnetii.

► *Seeing a picture of wild crinums flowering in flood water gave me the idea of taking large clumps of* Crinum x powellii *out of my borders, where their lank leaves are unduly obtrusive, and planting them in the shallow water near the margin of my horse pond (where the farm horses were led in to drink). The result has been exciting.*

been able to wrench it into a semblance of pink has been a major breeders' triumph, as witness no fewer than sixteen cultivars starting with 'Pink …' in the current issue of *The RHS Plant Finder*. Most are a muddy and uncomfortable colour. But if I wanted a pink day lily, I should settle either for the Award of Garden Merit-holding 'Stoke Poges' or for 'Fairy Tale Pink', both of which have been grown in an RHS trial.

Among the shrubby hebes, there are a good many with colourful flowers – purple, lavender, carmine, even crimson. Near to clear pink is 'Great Orme', the flowers fading on their spikes to near white, so that you have a bicolour effect. In 'Watson's Pink' (syn. 'Dorothy Peach') (1.8m/6ft), however, the numerous spikelets are clear pink throughout, in a great wave of blossom at the turn of June-July. I have grown the lavender-blue *Clematis* 'Prince Charles', over mine. Its flowers are not over-large but large enough to give definition to the hebe's haziness.

Incidentally, many clematis are described as pink, because they come nearer to that colour than to any other, but they are all tinged with more or less of blue. That includes the wide range of pink montana cultivars, derived from *C. montana* var. *rubens*. However, the camera is a great liar and more often than not represents clematis such as these as though they were true pink. The intending purchaser chooses accordingly and is then apt to complain to the supplier when the truth is revealed.

I must bring in hardy waterlilies (*Nymphaea*) at some point, so it might as well be here. It is best to choose by eye, as colour range among the pinks is considerable and could either please or disappoint you. I was disappointed by 'Marliacea Carnea', which is a weak, indefinite shade of pink, borne on a vigorous plant apt to take up a lot of space. 'James Brydon', of its kind, is excellent – bowl-shaped and a deep shade of carmine pink. For pure, clear pink I should recommend 'Rose Arey' (with rather spiky petals) or 'Perry's Pink'. Also 'Rose Magnolia', whose flowers are fairly pale but nicely shaped and offset by handsome foliage, each leaf quite deep bronze on the underside, which you appreciate when they stand a little out of the water.

A pink and grey bed or border could be a charming summer feature, soothing but definitely not exciting. I should enjoy planning it for you but shouldn't want it for myself. For grey, there will be lots of *Artemisia* 'Powis Castle' and *A. arborescens*. Also the unindented, broader grey leaves of *Plectranthus argentatus*. It is tender but bedding plants must be allowed. It is not difficult to

▲ A well-loved, spring-flowering perennial, Dicentra spectabilis (60cm/24in), lady's locket or lyre plant. The pink and white are perfectly combined in a gracefully presented flower. Seed is the readiest method of increase.

▼ Strong contrast in both colour and shape: the bright yellow Lily-flowered tulip 'West Point' with powerful carmine Bergenia 'Ballawley'. The bergenia's large, glossy leaves make a great setting.

think of other greys. In May-June, I have a very soft spot for the best pink forms of *Pimpinella major* 'Rosea', which is a native and totally undistinguished umbellifer when its usual white, but can be deep clear pink. It readily seeds itself, but the progeny need careful selection for depth of colouring.

In June-July, a delightful haze of pink will be provided by *Gypsophila paniculata* 'Flamingo' (90cm/36in); also, at the margin, by 'Rosenschleier' (30cm/12in) (Rosy Veil). Both are double. *Gaura lindheimeri* (90cm/36in) hovers, insect-like, for a couple of months in high summer. It is, overall, blush-white but its cultivar 'Siskiyou Pink' is a much deeper and more definite shade. We should certainly include the sidalceas mentioned above, as their spikiness is in valuable contrast to so much froth. And an excellent bedding verbena with an intertwangling habit, for the border's margin would be 'Silver Anne', which is a clear and definite shade of pink, only bleaching towards the end of its life.

All of this is very polite and in the best of taste, but will want pulling together somehow, with something more robust. I should suggest a rather glaucous-leaved and compact *Canna* called 'Erebus', with salmon-pink flowers, but not mawkishly coloured.

It seems to be axiomatic among the colour-sensitive, that pink and yellow are 'wrong'. (I've already shocked you with pink and orange on page 38.) This entirely ignores the fact that they are often seen together in the same flower. Thus, *Senecio elegans* is a smallish annual daisy that I enjoyed in South African springtime, with pink rays verging on carmine, a yellow disc and for good measure, lots of orange and yellow daisies like gazanias and arctotis flowering around it. This was in the wild and I would defy anyone to have disapproved. If you grew block of bright yellow next to block of bright pink, of course it would look horrid. But gardening doesn't have to be like that and we should keep an open mind at all times. (Naturally, I don't.)

In Beth Chatto's gravel garden, I was at one point confronted by the Spanish broom, *Spartium junceum*, flowering next to a bright carmine pink tree mallow, *Lavatera* 'Bredon Springs'. There was much else besides and the juxtaposition was not in the least aggressive, although both colours were strong, the broom's yellow bright but without the insistence of many brooms. 'I am always combining yellow and pink', Beth has told me on more than one occasion.

A combination that I enjoy in my own garden comes in

▼ *Following lupins, which I treat as expendable bedding plants, I followed up with limoniums (florists' statice) in pastel shades of pink, mauve and pale yellow. This tapestry seemed to lack substance, so we added bulbs of bright pink Nerine bowdenii, moved just before running up to flower, from clumps in other parts of the garden.*

autumn with a pink Japanese anemone – having a good deal of mauve in it, as they all do – growing in front of the 1.8m/6ft sunflower, *Helianthus* 'Lemon Queen'. That has masses of small, pale yellow daisies.

Nori Pope, in his garden at Hadspen, Somerset, is keen on colour theming; not on effective colour contrasting. On his nursery, what should turn up, in the clear pink bleeding heart, *Dicentra spectabilis*, but a mutation in which the young foliage accompanying the flowers, was yellow with only a touch of green! It has been named 'Gold Heart'. Naturally he has to be proud of it. Could he not now go the whole hog and show us that a pink and yellow border is on the cards?

**Anemone hupehensis
'Hadspen Abundance'**
Japanese anemone
Height: 1m/40in
Spread: 40cm/16in
Hardy, sun to light shade
A late summer- and
autumn-flowering perennial
with deep pink saucers and
a central knob of green
surrounded by a ring of
yellow stamens. Like the
pink form of A. x hybrida
(see 'White' page 122), it
looks good mingling with
Melianthus major or
beneath Rosa glauca.

Canna 'Erebus'
Height: 1.8m/6ft
Spread: 50cm/20in
Tender, sun
A stiffly erect plant with
large, glaucous, paddle-
shaped leaves and salmon
pink flowers in summer.
Looks handsome in front
of Acer negundo 'Flamingo'.

**Cleome hassleriana
(syn. C. spinosa)**
Spider flower
Height: 1.2m/4ft
Spread: 80cm/32in
Half-hardy annual, part
shade
A strongly structural
annual of almost shrub-like
habit, widely branching,
with handsome, palmate
hemp-like aromatic foliage.
Well nourished, damp soil.
Beware green spines at
base of leaf stalks. Flowers
without pause all summer
and autumn. ▶

Crepis incana
Pink dandelion
Height: 30cm/12in
Spread: 25cm/10in
Hardy, sun
Soft, clear pink dandelion-
like flowers appear in late
July, held above a rosette of
greyish leaves. It is
perennial but may be
short-lived and can be
propagated from root
cuttings or by division. It
needs good drainage and
an open, sunny position
but well-nourished soil.

Dianthus 'Inchmery'
Pink
Height: 23cm/9in
Spread: 23cm/9in
Hardy, sun
Flat, semi-double flowers
of a clear shell pink, held
above cushions of grey
foliage. Good at the front
of a border. It is well
scented, but being an old-
fashioned pink, flowers
only once, around
midsummer.

Dierama pulcherrimum ▲
Wand flower, angels'
fishing rods
Height: 2m/7ft
Spread: 2m/7ft
Near-hardy, full sun
Perennial, with iris-like
leaves and flexible but
steel-strong flowering
stems, looking best in fairly
isolated situations, such as
paving cracks. Self-sows.

Erythronium dens-canis
European dog's-tooth-violet
Height: 10cm/4in
Spread: 20cm/8in
Hardy, best in part-shade
An early spring-flowering
bulb, the petals reflexing in
daytime warmth, that will
flourish in thin turf. Beautiful,
purple-marbled foliage.
Split clumps immediately
after flowering. ▼

Gypsophila 'Rosenschleier'
Baby's breath
Height: 30cm/12in
Spread: 1m/40in
Hardy, sun
Still often known as 'Rosy
Veil', this has pale pink
double flowers and the
same airy way of flowering
as G. paniculata (see
'White' page 122) but it is
shorter and the plant is not
quite so strong. Happiest
on light soils. Good for the
front of a border, perhaps
with greenish yellow
Euphorbia seguieriana.

Hebe 'Great Orme'
Height: 1.2m/4ft
Spread: 1.2m/4ft
Hardy, sun
Forms a round bush with
glossy leaves, purple stems
and pink flowers in
summer and sometimes
again in autumn if the first
crop is dead-headed. As
the flower ages, the pink
fades to white giving a two-
tone effect. Try it with
Teucrium fruticans. H.
'Watson's Pink', with clear
pink flowers, looks good
with Artemisia ludoviciana
'Silver Queen' and Clematis
'Prince Charles'.

**Hyacinthus orientalis
'Anna Marie'**
Hyacinth
Height: 25cm/10in
Spread: 15cm/6in
Hardy, sun or light shade
Solid spires of soft pink
flowers appear in spring. It
is very fragrant. Plant
where it will not be
disturbed, as amongst
peonies or even roses. It is
also good for forcing for
indoors. Another good
pink variety is 'Lady Derby'.
Try it with Spiraea japonica
'Goldflame'.

Nymphaea 'Rose Arey'
Waterlily
Height: 15cm/6in
Spread: 1.5m/5ft
Hardy, sun
Star-shaped flowers with pointed petals of a pure pink. The central boss of stamens is golden. Other good pinks are 'Perry's Pink' or 'Rose Magnolia'. ◀

Papaver orientale 'Karine'
Oriental poppy
Height: 60cm/24in
Spread: 60cm/24in
Hardy, sun
Simple saucer-shaped, pure pink flowers, with dark basal spots. It flowers later than most oriental poppies and is fairly dwarf, scarcely needing support. An alternative is the frilly, pink 'Juliane'. Cut down after flowering and interplant with summer bedding.

Penstemon 'Evelyn'
Height: 60cm/24in
Spread: 30cm/12in
Hardy, sun or partial shade
Rose-pink racemes of narrow bells, paler on the inside, are carried elegantly above the narrow foliage. Take cuttings as a precaution, as it is not that long-lived.

Pimpinella major 'Rosea'
Height: 1.2m/4ft
Spread: 60cm/24in
Hardy, sun or partial shade
An umbellifer of the cow-parsley variety, but with rose-pink flower heads, which appear in early summer. It could be planted either in a border with June-flowering campanulas or in a meadow garden.

Rosa 'The Fairy'
Height: 1m/40in
Spread: 1m/40in
Hardy, sun
A small, compact rounded bush for the mixed border, with neatly double, clear pink Polyantha flowers over a long period from midsummer onwards. Plant *Viola cornuta* to scramble up through it.

Salvia involucrata 'Bethellii'
Sage
Height: 1.5m/5ft
Spread: 50cm/20in
A tuberous-rooted, nearly hardy perennial sage, safest if lifted in late autumn. Terminal flower racemes and ball-shaped knob of bracts in bright mauvey-pink ('shocking' pink), summer and autumn. Very striking. ◀

Schizostylis coccinea 'Mrs Hegarty'
Height: 30cm/12in
Spread: 50cm/20in
Hardy, sun
Colony-forming perennial, best split and replanted frequently. Must have moisture and an open site. Autumn-flowering. 'Jennifer' is the best pink clone and 'Major' the best red. 'Sunrise' is salmon-pink. ▼

Sidalcea 'Elsie Heugh'
Height: 75cm/30in
Spread: 45cm/18in
Hardy, sun
Spikes of saucer-shaped, clear pink flowers that bloom in the summer. This form is generally self-supporting. The taller 'Sussex Beauty', of the same colouring, will need support. Try with the *Delphinium* Belladonna hybrids or roses.

Tulipa 'China Pink'
Height: 50cm/20in
Spread: 15cm/6in
Hardy, sun
A Lily-flowered tulip with waisted flowers in a strong shade of pink, with flaring, pointed tips to the petals. Try it with blue forget-me-nots (*Myosotis*) or pink pomponette daisies (*Bellis*). ▶

Verbena 'Silver Anne'
Height: 30cm/12in
Spread: 60cm/24in
Tender, sun
Flat heads of soft pink flowers, fading to near white on a sprawling bedding verbena for the front of the border. It will climb around and through other plants, such as the variegated Virginia creeper, *Ampelopsis glandulosa* var. *brevipedunculata* 'Elegans'. It is perennial but usually treated as an annual and overwintered as cuttings.

Sunlit PURPLE

Purple is dark and rich. Imperial purple suggests velvet and the sumptuous. But I am very wary of deep purples in the garden. If they are to show up, you need to be close to them and with sunlight behind you.

If the flowers are large, as with dahlias and some clematis, they help themselves, but if small, they are easily lost. An all-purple border, unless relieved with touches of some other colour, is a mistake, especially in Britain, when we so often cower beneath grey skies. Purple will offer no relief. But in situations of contrast, there is plenty of scope.

Take the tall, autumn-flowering, American Joe Pye weed, *Eupatorium purpureum*. It has well-shaped, domed heads of dusty purple flowers, rather more intensely coloured in 'Atropurpureum'. It likes damp, so you might plant it beside water. Will it bring joy to your heart? Pretty limited joy, I should say, but then give it a tall and stately grass for a neighbour and see the transformation. *Miscanthus sinensis* 'Strictus' (1.8m/6ft) is of proudly upright habit, its upwards-pointing strap-leaves liberally cross-banded with yellow. They will give just the support that's needed and you might let them be joined, in October, by the white, green-eyed daisy, *Leucanthemella serotina* (*Chrysanthemum uliginosum*) (1.8m/6ft), or by white sprays of fragrant *Persicaria polystachya* (1.8m/6ft). (Beth Chatto plantings have inspired these thoughts.) Best if the scale was quite spacious. Throw in a gunnera – *G. tinctoria* or *G. manicata* – and the scene is set for many August to October weeks.

Another purple flower, again American, that I am fond of, late

◄ Clematis 'Victoria' is the perfect intermediary between the over-heavy purple of 'Jackmanii Superba' and the mauve-blue of 'Perle d'Azur'. It is of sufficiently strong colouring and no less agreeable as it fades. It has a long high-summer-flowering season on its young growth and can be hard pruned in winter. Nice with pink hybrid musk roses, if you can get them to coincide.

◀ *The strong, upright spikes of* Acanthus spinosus *have an excellent contrasting background in the prolific, midsummer-flowering Clematis 'Etoile Violette', at West Dean in Sussex. The white stamens in its flowers give them focus.*

▲ *The perennial* Verbascum chaixii *is normally yellow – this is the white variant – and has the surprising contrast of purple stamens. Easily propagated from root cuttings but also self-sows.*

▼ *Perennial moisture-lovers* Eupatorium purpureum *'Atropurpureum' contrasted with the white plumes of* Artemisia lactiflora.

in the season, is ironweed, *Vernonia crinita* (1.8m/6ft), a tall composite with compound flowering heads that are reddish purple all through. But not on its own and not with a dark background. It would go well with the gang I have just described but it was also good at the back of my one-sided Long Border, interplanted with the annual *Cosmos bipinnatus* 'Purity', with feathery green leaves and sizeable white daisies.

A purple-flowered shrub whose novelty thrilled me when it first appeared but of which I soon wearied was *Buddleja davidii* 'Royal Red'. It is more effective than 'Black Knight', which lacks any redness in its purple colouring, but is still singularly lifeless. I put this partly down to its aggressively boring foliage. The yellow-variegated sport from it, called 'Harlequin', is a lot livelier.

Any sort of mitigation of purple is helpful. *Dictamnus albus* var. *purpureus* is the dittany that I have seen wild in Hungarian woodland and it has stripy flowers in two shades of purple. That makes for agreeable variety, though I must add that the pure white dictamnus, whose panicles are seen against deepest, richest green foliage, is a far more effective plant.

Purple appears surprisingly at the centre of the flower spikes of perennial *Verbascum chaixii* (1.5m/5ft), which is typically bright yellow but may be pale yellow or white. Always, however, with softly hairy purple stamens. In crocuses, it is generally the orange stigmata that draw our attention when sited in the middle of a purple flower. Purple or deep blue makes an ideal setting for the brighter colour. This is noticeable in spring-flowering crocuses but even more so in the autumn-flowering *Crocus nudiflorus* and *C. speciosus*.

What makes you notice a plant or flower? As I said at the start, purple needs to be close to you if it is an unrelieved 'dead' purple. Thus, the Viticella-type *Clematis* 'Royal Velours', which arouses a good deal of excitement in many gardeners because it is so very dark, catches out my inattention over and over again. My specimen is a good one and flowers freely but not till Fergus points out to me that it is in flower do I notice it at all. Very well; I have placed it, admittedly quite close to a path, which is as it should be, but so that the light, for most of the day, comes from behind it. The mattness of the flower simply cannot compete.

Compare this with the deepest purple-leaved sumach, *Cotinus coggygria* 'Royal Purple'. You grow this entirely for the splendour of its foliage, to which end a hard cut-back each winter is the best recipe for producing plenty of young shoots with the handsomest

◄ ◄ We have had fun in our stock beds since grouping our plants rather than growing them in rows. Here, Penstemon 'Drinkstone' with purple Salvia x superba and pale yellow Achillea 'Lucky Break'. All strong colour contrasts and given a further lift by one plant in their midst of Verbascum chaixii, with yellow spires. Cardoon foliage on the left makes for firmness and solidity.

leaves. Height can be adjusted by your pruning but the bush needs to be tall enough so that, from a standing position, you can admire low sunlight (morning or evening) shining from behind it and translucently making every leaf it touches glow like precious stones.

Other cases of translucent purple foliage are to be found in certain cannas – *Canna indica* 'Purpurea', for instance. Its greeny-purple leaves stand almost erect and seem to be deliberately courting the dramatic effects of translucence at either end of the day. The purple-leaved strain of orach, *Atriplex hortensis* (1.8m/6ft) (related to spinach and edible itself) is effective both when seen translucently and with the light behind you; when in a colour harmony, as it might be behind the mauve border phlox, 'Princess Sturdza', or as a contrast, say to the green plumes of *Helianthus salicifolius* and the yellow daisies of *Telekia speciosa*.

The young shoots of herbaceous *Clematis recta* 'Purpurea' are striking in a spring border, not for their translucence but because of the intrinsic contrast in colour and texture between the front and the back of the leaves, both equally visible because largely held upright. The backs are quite pale with the soft down covering them. So are the young stems.

Larger purple flowers have a greater chance of drawing attention to themselves than if they are small. The luminous reddish-purple dahlia, 'Hillcrest Royal' (1.8m/6ft), is a Medium-cactus type, by no means large but it makes an eye-catching display. I have had it with the green mops of papyrus, *Cyperus papyrus* (1.8m/6ft), with a brilliantly white-variegated grass, *Arundo donax* var. *versicolor* (1.2m/4ft) and, in front, with the rich red racemes of *Lobelia* 'Queen Victoria' (90cm/36in). Sometimes I mix in another dahlia, like the small-decorative 'White Ballet' or red semi-double 'Bishop of Llandaff'.

The ever-popular *Clematis* 'Jackmanii Superba' starts with the advantage of producing solid blocks or sheets of a slightly reddish purple (the warmth of red helps). I have a column of it up a 3m/10ft pole at the back of my border, where it forms a background to bright yellow *Senecio doria* (1.8m/6ft) with flattish heads of small yellow daisies; and to the bright green columns of linear foliage borne by *Helianthus salicifolius* right through the summer.

'Etoile Violette' is another, slightly earlier-flowering (June on) clematis of the same type. There is nothing of red in its purple but it has a white eye, which greatly increases its impact. The flowering of 'Gipsy Queen' is concentrated on August and this is a slightly reddish purple all through, including the stamens. I never

▲ Lychnis coronaria
(75cm/30in) is a free self-
sower and will be found
flowering in all sorts of
unexpected places. Being
coloured magenta, the
flowers liven things up no
end. Here a plant is in the
centre of an as yet
unflowered colony of
Hedychium densiflorum.

▼ Magenta and lime-
green, with Geranium
psilostemon
'Bressingham Flair'
running through a colony
of the dwarf bamboo,
Pleioblastus auricomus,
at The Old Vicarage, East
Ruston, Norfolk.

saw it better displayed than when highlighted by a surrounding froth of the pure white *C. flammula*, an August-flowering species, with tiny, fragrant flowers.

I now want to move on from these typical purples to the much brighter colour known as magenta, which is purple with a strong dash of red admixed. Magenta is a town in northern Italy where a battle was won by the French against the Austrians in 1859 and the brilliant aniline dye that was synthesized shortly after took its name from that. It is quite a startling colour and therefore has many enemies among those who have difficulties with strong colours in general.

Typical are the flowers of *Lychnis coronaria*, which are moon-shaped on a plant providing its own appropriate background with grey stems and leaves. As usual, with a colour which scares, the breeders have busied themselves with modifications. There is 'Abbotswood Rose' (now *L.* x *walkeri*), in which the blue element is almost excluded; 'Alba', white; and 'Oculata', white with a pink eye. All are thin gruel compared with the type-plant.

There are splendid examples among the cranesbills. Just about as vivid a magenta as you can well imagine is found in *Geranium cinereum* var. *subcaulescens*, the colour highlighted by the flower's black centre. This is a small plant, hardly suited to general border use. For that purpose, turn to *G. psilostemon* (1m/40in), the peak of whose flowering season is in June. A rather bluer magenta than the last, it is still very bright and again has a black centre. Its habit is rangy; presented with neighbours taller than itself, it will hoist itself into them. I have a really bright early-summer combination with this as foreground to the tall, semi-double yellow buttercup, *Ranunculus acris* 'Stevenii' (1.2m/4ft) and the blood-red oriental poppy which I know as 'Goliath' (it is not the same as 'Beauty of Livermere'). There are plenty of softer-looking plants around to prevent undue abrasiveness.

'Ann Folkard' is a hybrid between this species and *G. procurrens*. It is a lovely bright purple but not quite magenta. It retains the black eye and from *G. procurrens* it inherits the habit of meandering, indefinite growth, so that its season, which starts in late May, continues for more than three months. One plant develops an extensive spread, which needs to be catered for, but it dies back at the end of the season to a modest crown. I like this next to the acid lime-green of *Euphorbia schillingii* (1.2m/4ft), which flowers July to September.

Magenta and green contrast so effectively that I should love to

The colour contrast in its surroundings of *magenta* Gladiolus communis *subsp.* byzantinus, *when introduced to a meadow setting, is amazingly lively.*

► *There have been many developments in colour and size of* Bougainvillea glabra, *but best of all, in my view, is the original magenta as you see it, in warm climates, draped over a whitewashed wall. Here at Great Dixter, we bed it out as a de-potted plant in the Exotic Garden.*

establish *G. psilostemon* in meadow turf, but have so far been only partially successful. Another magenta flower that looks splendid in a meadow setting is *Gladiolus communis* subsp. *byzantinus* (90cm/36in). In acquiring this, beware, because the dried corms offered by bulb specialists give rise to pinky-mauve flowers, not the strong magenta we are looking for (abundant in cottage gardens) at all. Beth Chatto offers the genuine article. I find that in grass it holds its own but does not increase. It is lovely under border conditions – really exciting when combined with the latest of all tulips, the scarlet *Tulipa sprengeri*. As the gladiolus makes up quickly in a border, you can transfer corms to your meadow on a fairly regular basis.

Dianthus carthusianorum (60cm/24in), with heads of magenta flowers at the top of virtually naked stalks, is a species that I greatly admired under meadow conditions in Romania but have failed to establish in my own meadow. Your conditions might be just right for it.

I do not want to leave the cranesbills without singing the praises of *Geranium* x *riversleaianum* 'Russell Prichard'. It is a bright, albeit bluish, magenta and I like to have it at a border's margin, where it can be allowed to surge forwards on to path or patio but can also filter backwards and upwards so as to thread its way into slightly taller neighbours. Its leaves are greyish green and softly hairy. I particularly like it where it is able to mix in with the grey stems and foliage of *Artemisia ludoviciana* 'Silver Queen'

▲ Petunia 'Purple Wave' is normally very low growing but, like many of its kind, it will rise to meet a challenge, in this case softening the stark sculptural outlines of Yucca gloriosa. They make strange but effective bedfellows.

(60cm/24in or more but adjustable). This geranium starts flowering in May and keeps on non-stop into October. Not surprisingly, perhaps, following the expenditure of so much energy, plants tend to die out after a few years but it is easy to take winter cuttings for replacement stock.

'Purple Wave' is a prostrate petunia that you raise from seed, which has won great popularity of recent years. It is magenta rather than purple, and, unlike many petunias, quickly recovers if it has been battered by heavy rain or hail. I grow colchicums in my borders as well as in the meadows. When their foliage has been cut down at the end of June, we interplant the clumps with a few plants of 'Purple Wave', which soon makes a complete carpet. This then forms a background to the pinky-mauve colchicums when they come up to flower in August-September.

Cistus x *purpureus* (1.2m/4ft) makes a large, loose shrub (you can keep it compact by clipping it over after its May-June flowering), and has fair-sized magenta flowers with darker blotches near the centre. I actually prefer *C.* x *pulverulentus* 'Sunset' (60cm/24in), a smaller, denser shrub with grey-green leaves and intense, solidly magenta flowers over a long period. We once grew the orange-flowered South African annual daisy, *Osteospermum hyoseroides*, in front of this and enjoyed the splash!

You sometimes find similar contrasts within one flower. Thus the not-too-amenable *Senecio pulcher* (45cm/18in), an autumn-flowering perennial (I'll get the length of its foot one day), has magenta daisies with large yellow discs. The annual *S. elegans* is much the same on a smaller scale.

I visited Fergus in the south of France when he was gardening there and admired a mixed daisy carpet of yellow gazanias and magenta 'mesembryanthemums', as we loosely term them – actually *Carpobrotus edulis*. At 9.00 in the morning, they were nothing, not having rubbed the sleep from their eyes, but by mid-morning, wow!

I love to see the typical magenta bougainvillea tumbling over whitewashed walls, in those warm countries. There are ever so many other bougainvillea colours available nowadays, all supposedly with a better pedigree, but none, in my opinion, to touch that magical magenta.

Whereas purple is a colour that greatly benefits from contrast, don't feel you have to be subtle in your use of magenta. It is apt to be brash but we are talking about flowers, after all, and their delicacy goes counter to brashness.

Allium hollandicum 'Purple Sensation'

Height: 1m/40in
Spread: 10cm/4in
Hardy, sun or part-shade
Late spring-flowering, bulbous allium. Will self-sow if undisturbed but can be lifted after flowering and replanted in fall. Rich purple globes, contrasting in shape with other purples and mauves: *Chaerophyllum hirsutum* 'Roseum', *Salvia sclarea* (foliage), *Silene dioica* 'Flore Pleno'.

Amaranthus hypochondriacus

Height: 2m/7ft
Spread: 1m/40in
Tender, sun
Late summer- and autumn-flowering annual for a sunny position in good soil. We save our own seed from this purple-leaved, purple-flowered form, which continues to perform after the purple form of orach, *Atriplex hortensis* var. *rubra*, has run to seed.
◄

Atriplex hortensis var. rubra

Red orach
Height: 1.8m/6ft
Spread: 60cm/24in
Hardy, sun
Fertile, moist, but free-draining soil.
An annual with deep purple foliage and an upright habit. It self-sows readily, often in ideal places. Try it with *Phlox paniculata* and *Astilbe chinensis* var. *taquetii* 'Superba' or contrasting with yellow *Verbascum olympicum*.

Cistus x pulverulentus 'Sunset'

Rock rose
Height: 60cm/24in
Spread: 1m/40in
Hardy, sun
A low, spreading shrub with grey-green leaves and magenta flowers over a long period. For a strong contrast, plant with the orange-flowered annual daisy, *Osteospermum hyoseroides*. A taller cistus with paler magenta colouring is *C.* x *purpureus*, but it is not so long in flower.

Clematis viticella 'Purpurea Plena Elegans'

Height: 3m/10ft
Spread: 1m/40in
Hardy, top in sun, roots in shade
Late flowering and one of the oldest double clematis of old rose colouring. 'Royal Velours' has small, deep velvety purple flowers in midsummer. 'Victoria' is later, with larger rosy-purple flowers. Planting dark clematis with the white *C. flammula* gives them a lift.
▼

Cotinus coggygria 'Royal Purple'

Smoke bush
Height: 5m/15ft
Spread: 5m/15ft
Hardy, sun
A deciduous shrub grown mainly for its leaves; dark purple in summer and scarlet in autumn. Cut back in winter to improve the foliage but the airy plumes of minute flowers will be lost. Plant with evening or morning sunlight shining from behind. The almost fluorescent green flowers of *Veratrum viride* show up well against the cotinus's foliage.

Dahlia 'Hillcrest Royal'

Height: 1.8m/6ft
Spread: 60cm/24in
Tender, sun
A Medium cactus dahlia with rolled petals giving a spiky appearance. The colour is rich reddish purple. Good with the variegated grass *Arundo donax* var. *versicolor* and red *Lobelia* 'Queen Victoria'.

Dianthus carthusianorum

Carthusian pink
Height: 40cm/16in
Spread: 20cm/8in
Hardy, sun
A pink with long stems and small magenta flowers in dense heads. Early summer flowering. It grows in grassland but does best on free-draining banks. Try it in light, well-drained soil with *Artemisia* 'Powis Castle'.

Dictamnus albus var. purpureus

Dittany
Height: 1m/40in
Spread: 60cm/24in
Hardy, sun or partial shade
Panicles of butterfly-like flowers, striped in two shades of purple, and dark green, lemon-scented foliage. The developing, winged seedpods are also handsome. Do not plant with other purples or it will deaden the colour.

Eupatorium purpureum

Joe Pye weed
Height: 1.8m/6ft
Spread: 1m/40in
Hardy, sun
Purple stems and domed heads of dusty purple flowers much loved by butterflies. Its cultivar 'Atropurpureum' is even darker in colour. It looks good next to a tall grass, *Miscanthus sinensis* 'Strictus', for example, or with yellow, green-coned *Rudbeckia* 'Herbstsonne' and creamy plumes of *Artemisia lactiflora*.

Geranium psilostemon
Armenian cranesbill
Height: 1m/40in
Spread: 1m/40in
Hardy, sun
Bright magenta flowers in early summer, each with a black eye. It forms a large mound. *G.* 'Ann Folkard' is similar but smaller (60cm/24in) and the leaves are yellowish when they first appear. Try these and the similarly coloured *G. x riversleaianum* 'Russell Prichard' (but with grey-green leaves) near oranges, yellows and reds to get a dazzling combination of colours, or next to lime-greens for a more subtle association.

Geranium sanguineum
Bloody cranesbill
Height: 30cm/12in
Spread: 45cm/18in
Hardy, sun
Deeply cut leaves and flat magenta flowers that appear over most of the summer and into autumn. Nice threaded through the glaucous foliage of the grass *Helictotrichon sempervirens. G. s.* 'Shepherd's Warning' is an even more brilliantly coloured cultivar.

Gladiolus communis
subsp. *byzantinus*
Height: 1m/40in
Spread: 15cm/6in
Hardy, sun
A tall stem of bright magenta flowers in the late spring and early summer. It self-sows and multiplies readily in border conditions.

Lychnis coronaria
Rose campion
Height: 90cm/3ft
Spread: 60cm/24in
Hardy, sun
A branching perennial with grey, felted stems and leaves which contrast with the brilliant magenta flowers. It is short-lived, but readily self-sows. It can be calmed with a soft planting or made even brasher by planting with *Crocosmia* 'Lucifer'.

Petunia 'Purple Wave'
Height: 30cm/12in
Spread: 45cm/18in
Tender, sun
This magenta-coloured petunia is little affected by rain as so many cultivars are. It is low-growing and spreading. Plant over autumn-flowering colchicums which will flower through the petunia.

Vernonia crinita
Ironweed
Height: 1.8m/6ft
Spread: 75cm/30in
Hardy, sun
Heads of rich purple flowers, each individual flower being quite small. It is late into growth. Try it with the white-flowered *Cosmos bipinnatus* 'Purity'.

Malope trifida 'Vulcan'
Mallow
Height: 90cm/3ft
Spread: 70cm/28in
Tender, sun and average soil
Of the annual mallows, 'Vulcan' has the richest colouring. We like to sow late spring for late summer effect. Green slits at the base of the flower are formed by the enclosing calyx and are translucent, like stained glass.

Orchis mascula
Early purple orchid
Height: 30cm/12in
Spread: 15cm/6in
Hardy, open site
The native British early purples (of Shakespeare) are tuberous-rooted perennials, happy in open woodland or meadow, flowering in April, with a rank smell of tom cat. Often seen along road verges. Handsomely purple-spotted foliage. *Dactylorhiza foliosa*, for part shade among *Polystichum* ferns, has long spikes of purple flowers.

BROWN Studies

In the outside world, brown is the symbol of dying or dead plants. It is the antithesis of living green. But brown can be full of vitality. And what of that essential component of life, the soil?

When the earth is dark brown, we feel pleased. Moisture is there and nourishing organic matter. On pruning our deciduous shrubs, the colour of their stems is most important. Dark brown is synonymous with young wood that is full of energy. Pale beige stems have been around a while and these are the ones that we shall remove when rejuvenating a bush and admitting light to its centre so as to encourage the production of young growth.

The warm, gleaming brown of young bark in certain trees is a principal reason for growing them. The cherry *Prunus serrula* has rather miserable little whitish flowers but the bark, which has been newly exposed by peeling off the old layer, is shining reddish brown and most attractive. The maple *Acer griseum* is another famed example. Old bark flakes off and you can 'help' it by rubbing the stem so that more of the new is exposed. Which is why we are often encouraged to site the tree where it is close to a frequent route of passage, encouraging us to give it this physical attention, so satisfying to the giver.

When a woman's hair is flatteringly referred to as chestnut brown, I do not know whether it is the horse or the sweet chestnut which is being referred to, but it could be the fruit of either as it appears when first revealed, newly released from the prickly husk which enclosed it. Another case of tactile pleasure, just to feel this smooth and beautiful object between our fingers.

◄ *The seed heads of thistles, especially when ripe, are hygroscopic. Whenever there is a dry wind in winter or early spring, they open out like a living flower, as here with our carline thistle, Carlina* vulgaris. *It is an easily cultivated biennial but grows wild on thin, limy soils. Since it cannot be relied upon to self-sow, you need to collect seed and sow in a pot.*

▲ *One of the attractions of many fritillaries is their murky, subfusc colouring, in this case* Fritillaria pyrenaica *(41cm/16in), which is an easy species in cultivation, taking readily to border life. Here it is with grape hyacinths,* Muscari armeniacum 'Blue Spike'.

Seeing that brown stalks and leaves are perfectly natural transition colours, there is no need to resent them, provided we accept the natural cycle of the seasons. When they do become objectionable, the fault is most often with us for having bred ever-larger blooms that are generally packed with a superabundance of petals. This is the case with many double camellias. Their double-ness has lost them the capacity of freely shedding their flowers when they have been wind-bruised, frosted or simply run their natural course. They remain appallingly apparent on the bush.

It is the same with double roses. Many are borne in trusses with buds at different stages of development. When the most precocious have flowered, instead of dropping their petals, they hold on to them in a brown condition, ruining the display which later-opening buds would otherwise provide. Dead-heading in these circumstances would be such a niggle that it simply is not practical. Yet the doters on roses seem to be entirely blind to the defects of their darlings; if you dare to criticize the rose, they take it as a personal affront (perhaps it can be!).

Dead-heading rhododendrons is a great performance where they are grown on a large scale, involving ladder work and a lot of time. The excuse given is that seed setting would prejudice the next year's flowering. I have closely observed this question and I can state with confidence that whether or not you dead-head, the out-come will be the same. The real, although unstated, reason for this chore is that the dead, unshed blooms of many rhododendrons (not all, by any means) are an appalling sight which cannot be tolerated.

A curious example of brownness is in the overall brown cast on the majority of New Zealand plants. I have heard it mooted that this is a protection against the sun's burning quality, because the 'hole' in the ozone layer in those parts is of very long standing and is by no means a recent phenomenon. The plants react as humans do with suntan. Be that as it may, New Zealand plants are a fascinating ingredient-with-a-difference in our British gardens. When a visitor says, disparagingly, of my *Carex buchananii* (60cm/24in), which is a grass-like sedge, 'is that alive or dead?', I think to myself, 'you're a pretty poor judge of the difference between the quick and the dead'. The healthy gleam that is reflected from the plant's foliage could only belong to a living plant.

A New Zealand shrub that both Fergus and I are dotingly fond of (though it is largely ignored by the public, I must admit) is *Olearia solandri*. Of rather upright habit to some 2.4m/8ft, it is a mass of tiny brownish leaves which contrast strikingly with their

▲ *In our Peacock Garden, the topiary birds have been newly clipped in early autumn and make a firm setting for looser plants, notably of the Far Eastern grass genus, Miscanthus, seen flowering here. M. sinensis has a great range of selected cultivars and their colouring changes as their flower heads develop, often from rich brown, gradually to pale fawn. They last in beauty till the new year, in many cases. Double hedges of the bushy Michaelmas daisy, Aster lateriflorus 'Horizontalis' (60cm/24in), are nearing their climax, with a haze of purplish pink linking the topiary peacocks.*

lusher surroundings. The whole shrub, at any time of the year, gives off an aroma of heliotrope, which stops you in your tracks when your thoughts were probably elsewhere. In August, it briefly erupts into a seething mass of insignificant white flowers, and the heliotrope scent is then stronger still. This shrub seeds itself around and I am flattered.

The last New Zealand example from my garden, *Libertia peregrinans* (45cm/18in), already mentioned as a companion to orange tulips, really does attract attention. An evergreen perennial, it has stiff, narrow linear leaves, rather like some irises, and they are a murky brownish green but their prominent midrib is orange-brown, especially bright in winter. They make a colony at the front of my Long Border. I grow other libertia species, such as *L. formosa,* but they hail from South America and are dark green-leaved without a hint of brown.

Not many of my examples of brown are combined with another colour, but there is a striking contrast in some magnolias. The furry bracts which enclose the flower buds are usually some dusky shade of green but in most white-flowered magnolias they are very dark brown. As the bud expands into a bloom, the enclosing bracts have to yield to the pressures from within, and we can admire a snowy whiteness on the expanding bloom contrasted with brown on the bracts alongside.

Another example of brown and white working in happy

▲ *Hoar frost highlighting the pale flower heads of* Miscanthus sinensis *'Undine'.*

◀◀ *The pyramidal seed heads of* Sinacalia tangutica *(formerly* Senecio tanguticus*) are almost as beautiful in December as the spidery yellow flowers in August and September (see page 139). Branches of the old fig that preceded my family at Dixter have lost their leaves but the undeveloped fruit persists.*

contrast is in a show auricula – a group of florists' flowers in which the West Yorkshire Craven Nursery specializes – called 'Brownie'. Auriculas are a branch of the primrose tribe, in which the thick leaves are rather fleshy. In this case they are overlaid with a thin floury coating, which is a sought-after feature. 'Brownie's perfectly circular flowers are warm brown in an outer zone, which surrounds a white eye. Show auriculas are always container-grown. This cultivar makes a beautiful, large specimen when grown in a terracotta pan, the trunk-like stems below its leafy rosettes becoming woody with age.

A very living and attractive brown is widely admired in the fruits of medlars, which are not quite smooth but have a kind of bumpily speckled surface. Other fruits are similar to this albeit on a smaller scale; for instance those of the wild and domestic service trees, *Sorbus torminalis* and *S. domestica*.

The attraction of many ornamental grasses in winter is in their pale brown presence, which is retained intact without being unduly battered. The cultivars of *Miscanthus sinensis* will generally hold on at least till the new year, sometimes longer. *Stipa calamagrostis* (1m/40in) is one of the best, retaining its inflorescence as well as its stems, all arching in the direction opposite to the prevailing wind's. *Calamagrostis* x *acutiflora* 'Karl Foerster' (1.8m/6ft), which is all soft fluffiness and purple when flowering in June-July, turns pale beige in October and is reduced to pale, bleached stems in winter, upright as stair rods and remaining a beautiful feature till March, when I at last feel the time has come to cut them down and make way for next season's performance.

Hakonechloa macra 'Aureola' (30cm/12in) is beautiful in different ways for three quarters of the year: first with its pungent lime-green spears, in April, then to a settled green-and-yellow stripiness in summer, flowering warmly light brown in autumn and subsequently keeping us happy well into winter. Among a colony, *Spartina pectinata* 'Aureomarginata' with yellow-edged blades gives it a lift, being three times as tall (1m/40in).

Among the composites, some make especially beautiful flower skeletons, often remaining hygroscopic – the inflorescence closes sulkily in wet weather but fully expands when winds turn dry, often from the northeast in late winter. In fact, I am reluctant to cut down *Serratula seoanei* in March or even April, to make room for new growth, as the miniature, pale fawn-coloured flower heads from the previous autumn are so appealing. It is a kind of

▲ *Photographed in November, Miscanthus sinensis 'Silberfeder' (Silver Feather) is one of the most reliable of the older cultivars, always in flower by early September. The flower heads become bleached and fluffy as they age, but lose none of their charm.*

▼ *Possibly the longest-serving grass in my garden is Calamagrostis x acutiflora 'Karl Foerster'. Its purple fluffiness in early summer gradually settles down to pale fawn rods, here highlighted in November by a fruiting spindleberry, Euonymus europaeus.*

knapweed, and already a pleasure in summer, with its wiry tangle of dark, finely divided foliage. The small purple flower heads are at their best in October and look nice with the pink *Schizostylis coccinea* 'Viscountess Byng', which is also a late flowerer.

The wild carline thistle, *Carlina vulgaris*, is biennial, which entails frequent re-sowing, but well deserves the effort. In the wild, starvation conditions may produce only three flower heads to a plant, but under cultivation you can expect thirty, well spaced on a handsomely branching plant (45cm/18in). This is silver-grey when flowering, becoming beige in winter and retaining its shape right through to spring.

Few of our native trees turn to brilliant shades of scarlet or gold as do so many American and Japanese species, but their russet colours have their own charm, so I do not think we need to feel envious. Beeches (*Fagus sylvatica*) take on beautiful, glowing, bright brown shades. Whereas beech trees then shed their leaves, when clipped as hedges, the leaves are retained till young foliage pushes them aside the following April. The winter shade of brown is pale and many people count it as a virtue. I have to say I find its lifelessness rather depressing. I would rather have a bare hedge, like quickthorn (*Crataegus laevigata*), which starts greening up quite early in March. And a thick hedge of it will still retain privacy and filter most of the wind. Wind in a beech hedge rustles disconsolately. 'Keen, fitful gusts are whispering here and there among the bushes, half leafless and dry', to quote Keats. They do not create a cheerful mood.

Natural, seasonable browns are very welcome. I love the dark shapes of teazels (*Dipsacus fullonum*, 2m/7ft) in winter. They have a statuesque presence in many parts of our garden. But I reduce the numbers that are allowed in summer, drastically. They flower in early August – bands of mauve around their cones – but the plant then quickly becomes dead-looking to a degree that seems premature. The warm bronzes of chrysanthemums are just right for the season and their slightly acrid smell goes with it too, but we are not yet ready for sombrely dead-looking teazels. Hence a fairly drastic thinning out takes place. Later, when everything else is dead, we shall be glad of those teazels that remain.

So brown has an important place in our outdoor environment. It divides itself into two categories: living brown, full of vitality, and dead brown, making a passive, almost ghostly contribution. No one, surely, would forgo the sensual delight of shuffling their feet through a carpet of dead leaves. I certainly have not lost it.

Acer griseum
Paper-bark maple
Height: 6m/20ft
Spread: 3m/10ft
Hardy, sun
A well-shaped maple with attractive bark which, once it is more than three years old, peels like paper, showing a lighter colour beneath. Plant where the tree is within easy reach so that the bark can be rubbed when passing.
◄

Calamagrostis x acutifolia 'Karl Foerster'
Feather reed grass
Height: 1.8m/6ft
Spread: 60cm/24in
Hardy, sun
An elegant grass with subtly purple flower panicles in summer; the stems turn pale beige in autumn (nice with late dahlias), become paler and remain in good condition until the spring. The variegated 'Overdam' is good as a single upright feature.

Carex buchananii
Leatherleaf sedge
Height: 60cm/24in
Spread: 75cm/30in
Hardy, sun
A clump-forming grass-like sedge with glistening brown arching leaves. It looks good in paving cracks, self-sowing freely.

Carlina vulgaris
Carline thistle
Height: 45cm/18in
Spread: 30cm/12in
Hardy, sun
A biennial thistle with silvery rays around a large, pale brown disc. When well grown, on good soil and in full sun, it branches freely. *C. acaulis* is similar but with bigger flowers, also in July, on short, non-branching stems.

Dipsacus fullonum
Teazel
Height: 2m/7ft
Spread: 75cm/30in
Hardy, sun
A biennial with curious cupped leaves that hold water. It develops into a see-through candelabrum which turns brown to create fine silhouettes for the winter garden.
◄

Hakonechloa macra 'Aureola'
Height: 30cm/12in
Spread: 45in/18in
Hardy, sun or partial shade
A grass with green and yellow variegation that gradually changes to beige, in autumn, when it produces light brown flowers. It contributes warmly to the scene until the New Year, when it may be cut down. Good with *Spartina pectinata* 'Aureomarginata'.

Hydrangea anomala ►
subsp. petiolaris
Climbing hydrangea
Height: indefinite
Spread: indefinite by self-layering
Hardy, moist leaf soil in sun or shade
Deciduous, self-clinging climber, which can also be grown as an ordinary, independent shrub. Young stems in winter are warm, glossy brown, terminated by pale green buds at the tip. Abundant white lacecap blossom, early summer. Bright yellow fall colour.

Libertia peregrinans
Height: 45cm/18in
Spread: 30cm/12in
Hardy, sun
A stiff-leaved plant with brownish green foliage with an orange rib down the centre, which shows particularly well in winter. The flowers are white and appear in the early summer. Its upright spears contrast well with orange tulips and, in autumn, with the dwarf, mat-forming *Aster ericoides* f. *prostratus* 'Snow Flurry'.

Olearia solandri
Daisy bush
Height: 2.4m/8ft
Spread: 2m/7ft
Hardy, sun
An evergreen shrub with small heather-like brownish leaves smelling of heliotrope. White flowers appear in profusion in late summer, followed by brownish seed heads.

Prunus serrula
Cherry
Height: 10m/30ft
Spread: 8m/24ft
Hardy, sun
A well-shaped tree, grown for its attractive bark which peels in bands to reveal new shining bark of a rich coppery brown. Plant where the sun can strike the trunk. ▼

Serratula seoanei
Sawwort
Height: 45cm/18in
Spread: 30cm/12in
Hardy, sun
Finely-cut purplish foliage and small mauve-purple thistle heads in October, which last for months and in dry spring weather open to look like fresh brown flowers. ►

Sophisticated BLACK

'Invention flags, the mind grows muddy,
And black despair succeeds brown study.'

William Congreve

◀ *Black has many manifestations in our gardens, not least in fruit — privet berries, for instance, and the berries of* Fatsia japonica, *as also of ivy,* Hedera helix, *which is its close relation. These last do not ripen till the spring — fatsias in May. If the seeds are sown immediately, they will germinate forthwith.*

'Black has a bad press', Fergus remarks, as I quote this to him while he makes up my very comforting and far from black fire before leaving the room.

Black is associated with night, darkness, a heightened perception of sounds and grisly interpretations of them. Black menaces us with the unknown. Yet in Wagner's *Tristan and Isolde*, night and darkness is what the protagonists long for and it is unsympathetic day which menaces, with all its jealousies and misunderstandings between humans.

Black plays a major role in our clothing. It is the ideal antithesis with white in men's evening wear: a large area of black jacket, trousers and tie, contrasted with a little of glaring white in shirt and cuffs (plenty of which should show). When men don white evening clothes in summer, it is supposed to keep them cool, but is visually ineffective.

If men wear black, it is a kind of uniform intended to be in total contrast to what we wish to see women wearing. Ladies who relapse into their little black dress to avoid standing out in a crowd, risk being ignored. No one should want that.

In flowers and plants, black as a living colour is comparatively rare, but it is glamorous and sophisticated and therefore greatly to be desired. In its negation of light it is yet a highlight, especially if it has a reflecting gloss.

▲ The dusky purple flowers of Fritillaria persica 'Adiyaman' make a very black impression. They form a spike on top of a hefty stem of green foliage, blooming in April and sure of causing a mild sensation.

▼ Hollyhocks, Alcea rosea (2.4m/8ft), have a striking black version, 'Nigra', the colouring emphasizing the whiteness of the flower's centre. Black flowers always awaken the public's attention.

If few flowers are naturally black, we do our utmost to breed more of them to come as close to black as we can get. Black hellebores, for instance, of the *Helleborus orientalis* style. These do not show up in the garden at all, but when looked at closely, you gain a heightened impression of their pale stamens. Any botanical name with *niger* or *ater* in it denotes blackness; as *nigricans* = becoming black, near to black, or *atropurpureus* = blackish purple. So it is a little confusing that *niger* in *Helleborus niger*, the Christmas rose, which patently has white flowers, refers to the blackness of its roots.

Black intrigues; it arouses curiosity. I can see no other reason for growing the cranesbill species, *Geranium phaeum*, whose little black flowers, normally seen under woodland conditions which it prefers, but which swallow it up even more than would anyway be inevitable, are totally insignificant, yet have a great following in the gardening world. Not mine; display is my watchword, but I recognize that there are those who like to peer. Black flowers are for them, but we must not expect the garden of a peerer to make a great overall impression (unless of overall messiness).

Many an amateur has had a stab at growing *Fritillaria persica* 'Adiyaman' (75cm/30in). Above a heavy foundation of stem and grey leaves (it often snaps off at ground level in its windy spring season), is a raceme of disproportionately small bell-flowers, greyish on the outside, black within. It certainly looks 'different'.

Violas 'Molly Sanderson' and 'Bowles' Black' have been selected for their blackness; it is not natural to *Viola*. Most 'black' flowers are very dark purple. Such is *Veratrum nigrum*, a six-footer with beautifully pleated, bright green leaves in early spring (adored by slugs, alas), above which rises a candelabrum of deepest maroon star-flowers. They combine well in dappled shade with rich orange lilies, such as *Lilium pardalinum*. To be shown (I would hardly venture to say 'to own') a healthy colony of dark veratrum species in full July regalia does take your breath away. Even so, as an effective garden plant, I would settle for the white equivalent, *V. album*, every time.

Iris chrysographes (50cm/20in) has a natural slant towards black, greatly encouraged by the breeders. Thus we find 'Black Beauty', 'Black Knight', 'Black Velvet' and 'Kew Black' as cultivar names or simply unadorned black. Grow them in a boggy situation near to a brightly coloured candelabra primula and they look pretty good.

Black hollyhocks, *Alcea rosea* 'Nigra', can be telling, either with

▲ *In this annual climber,* Rhodochiton atrosanguineus, *the lantern-like calyx is purple and persists for weeks, whereas the tubular corolla is black and lasts only a short while. The dark trail of flowers is here highlighted (this was not organized; it did it itself) by the distinctive stripy leaves of* Canna 'Striata'.

▲ *The very dark pincushion flowers of sweet scabious,* Scabiosa atropurpurea *'Ace of Spades', form a charming background to the stamens' white anthers. This is usually treated as an annual, but sometimes does a second year.*

paler kinds or associated with something like a tall yellow mullein (*Verbascum*). This hollyhock's flower has, besides, a pale centre in its protruding cone of stamens.

I have a great affection for the annual or short-lived perennial sweet scabious, *Scabiosa atropurpurea* (90cm/36in) when, as its name suggests but is seldom realized in commercial practice, its flowers really are very, very dark. The 'Ace of Spades' strain, which I like to mix into my borders, has been selected for this attribute. The attraction is greatly heightened by the white peppering of each flower's anthers, this giving rise to the popular name pincushion flower.

Another flower in which you find this contrast is *Rhodochiton atrosanguineus*. This is generally treated as an annual climber (it will, in fact, survive a mild winter). It makes garlands of pendent, purple lampshade-like flowers, this persistent 'shade' being its calyx. Within it, however, but much more ephemeral, hangs a tubular corolla – pure black, I promise. The tube opens a little at the mouth, to reveal pure white anthers. You need to be close and in a peering mood to see, let alone enjoy, this contrast, but my main point would be that the entire garland, black or purple, is a pretty and effective feature. Not so *Salvia discolor*, although it gets some of my friends excited. It is a small shrub, flowering in early summer, but you need to have it pointed out to you that it is in flower. The calyx is green; only the little corolla is black. Barely a talking point, I should have said.

Black as part of an otherwise contrastingly coloured flower can be a winning situation, as in the annual ladybird poppy, *Papaver commutatum* (see page 17). Some of the oriental poppies have black petal bases, notably in *P. orientale* 'Black and White'.

We are straining to get a black dahlia. The nearest to it that I have yet seen is 'Dark Secret', which also happens to be a pretty plant (how lucky). It is quite small, with deeply cut, lacy foliage. The flowers are single, near to black and with deep yellow florets and stamens comprising the central disc. I have only seen this on the show bench but hope to own it some day.

For many years, everyone's darling has been the cocoa-scented *Cosmos atrosanguineus* (45cm/18in). It is tuberous-rooted and looks so like a dahlia to me that I suspect it of being a changeling. It fetched a lot of money until it was found to be an easy subject for micropropagation. Once settled in (I have failed to overwinter it on several attempts), it is a pretty reliably hardy perennial. But the actual plant is a weedy-looking affair which I have ceased to

covet (interpret that as you like).

Quite a number of purplish-black-flowered plants are strongly scented, whether pleasantly or not. The above-described sweet scabious has a musty sort of sweetness. The flowers of *Pittosporum tenuifolium* (6m/20ft), a shrub/tree of borderline hardiness, open in May and are the colour of bitter chocolate. They are night-scented and rather rankly in a chocolatey vein. The climber, *Akebia quinata*, is another such. You hardly notice its flowers aside from the scent. The dragon arum, *Dracunculus vulgaris*, has a deep purple spathe but the spadix (or club) is black. This smells of bad meat, thereby attracting pollinating blowflies.

Some flowers have black anthers, in marked contrast to the overall picture. The February-flowering *Rhododendron* 'Seta' (1.5m/5ft), with pink blossom that almost obliterates its sharp little leaves, is black-anthered and there are ten of them in each flower. You notice them. I also have a white-flowered agapanthus which is given chic by its black anthers. More often, black is an accessory: the black eye-like cones in otherwise rich yellow rudbeckias or the black centre in the typically orange flowers of *Thunbergia alata*, also known as black-eyed Susans.

Often it is some other part of a plant, its stems or leaves, that provides a strikingly black contrast to the rest. The black leaves of the celandine *Ranunculus ficaria* 'Brazen Hussy' are an ideal background to the vivid yellow flowers. I introduced this popular celandine. It was growing wild in a wood nearby and I had been aware of it there for years, before my Dutch friend, Romke van de Kaa, who was my head gardener at the time, suggested bringing it into the garden's sphere.

In *Ophiopogon planiscapus* 'Nigrescens', a lowish, strap-leaved plant, there is nothing but blackness, the only relief being provided by a light-reflecting gloss. How to use it is always the question. One popular wheeze is to interplant with white snowdrops, but these have a very limited season and are followed by weeks of lank green foliage; then nothing. As this ophiopogon has a slightly running habit, it lends itself rather well to paving cracks, with the paving (of high quality, naturally) providing a light background. Or you can plant it next to another runner of similar habit, as I have seen it with the green fronds of the New Zealand fern, *Blechnum penna-marina*. The two will blend and overlap at their interface. This sort of arrangement always requires surveillance, lest one partner overwhelms the other. Perfect matches are made only in heaven.

▲ *Flowers of the dragon arum,* Dracunculus vulgaris, *would stand out in any colour but the lurid combination of black spadix against a purple spathe, settles it. This aroid is hardy. Divide and replant the tubers soon after flowering, every other year, to ensure abundant flowering, in July, after which the plant rapidly withers.*

▶▲ *Sometimes it is a tiny feature, like the ten black anthers in each flower of this February-flowering* Rhododendron 'Seta' *(1.2m/4ft), that sets the seal of individuality.*

◀◀ *The excitingly dark, shovel-shaped leaves of* Colocasia esculenta *'Black Magic' will still be almost invisible unless you can somehow highlight them. I have used two white-variegated foliage plants:* Plectranthus madagascariensis *'Variegated Mintleaf' at the lower level and the variegated giant reed grass,* Arundo donax *var.* versicolor, *at the higher.*

▶ *We are as likely to take notice of a black eye in a sunflower (annual* Helianthus *'Valentine') as we would in a human.*

This ophiopogon is an extreme case. Another such is *Colocasia esculenta* 'Black Magic' (1.1m/44in). It is a tender perennial that can be bedded out or plunged into a pond, in summer. Belonging to the arum family, it has hastate leaves, like many aroids. I have not seen it attempting to flower, but leaves and leaf stalks are black and they reflect little light. The best way to show it off that I have found is with white-variegated foliage. I plant (or have planted) the grass, *Arundo donax* var. *versicolor*, which has broad white stripes, behind it and the spreading, green-and-white *Plectranthus forsteri* 'Marginatus' in front.

There is a well-named coleus called 'Inky Fingers'. *Solenostemon* is the correct name for this genus of, largely, foliage plants in many mixed Joseph Coat colours. They are tender and usually pot-grown but fun to plant out for the summer. 'Inky Fingers' has green leaves with black tips.

In the Japanese *Kirengeshoma palmata* (1.2m/4ft), stems and main leaf veins are black, but the interestingly shaped leaf blade is green and the open-tubed flowers are pale yellow. As in other contexts, black adds class. The same situation, albeit on a fairly mundane native wild plant, is found in the variety of cow parsley

▲ *An old Hortensia variety of* Hydrangea macrophylla, *'Nigra', that has always been distinctive by reason of its black stems. They still show up in winter, when the leaves have gone and the buns are brown. We do not prune till March.*

Anthriscus sylvestris called 'Ravenswing'. The flowers are white but the dissected leaves are verging on black.

The bugbane called *Cimicifuga simplex* var. *simplex* Atropurpurea Group (1.8m/6ft) has very dark leaves and stems in marked contrast to its spikes of white flowers. It is permanently in evening dress and commands a price in keeping with its status. I should warn that nurserymen, for speed and availability, tend to raise stock from seed, which gives mixed results (hence 'Group' in its naming). Ostensibly they select from the seedlings only those with the darkest leaves, but we all know about human nature being what it is. Having a see-through nature, this species is often suitable at a border's margin, perhaps with deep-blue aconites behind.

The bamboo *Phyllostachys nigra* gives us expectations of a green leaf smartly contrasting with black stems. The effect can be truly noble but is seldom realized in practice. You will not find all-black culms (canes) in any of the best known selections such as *punctata*, *henonis* or 'Boryana'. In some cases, the culms will blacken with age, say in four years, but if you like to thin your bamboos out on a regular basis, as I do, removing the oldest culms and leaving the youngest and most vigorous, you will be in a tight situation. Best if you can procure a plant with the habit of making black culms when they are still young. Such is forma *nigra*, offered by P. W. Plants, and they have an excellent bamboo record.

The black stems in a few shrubs are best appreciated in winter, when there are no leaves. Such is *Hydrangea macrophylla* 'Nigra', an old cultivar, with smallish Hortensia bun-heads in pink or light blue, but reliably borne and in profusion. Even at flowering, the stems remain significant.

Then there is the black-stemmed dogwood, *Cornus alba* 'Kesselringii'. Why bother? you might wonder, when we have the far more luminous red-stemmed kinds and the bright yellowy-green-stemmed *C. stolonifera* 'Flaviramea'. But if you have all three in adjacent groups with some white-stemmed birches behind, as I have seen them in a 1920s planting at Herstmonceux Castle, in East Sussex, you will certainly be stopped in your tracks.

Final manifestation of black in the plant world: black berries, including blackberries of the wild kinds that I love to go picking in the autumn. The notion that birds prefer red berries to those of any other colour – yellow, orange, pink, blue or black – dies hard and, in my observation, has no foundation in fact. Our breeders have selected certain colour aberrations, as in yellow-fruited

▲ Among green aeoniums and other succulents, the shiny black leaves of Aeonium 'Zwartkop' have no difficulty in drawing attention to themselves. These are fun to bed out for the summer. Here, they are in a hot, sunny border that we keep on the dry side. Sometimes, they wilt in the sun but perk up again quickly.

hollies, for the sake of variety. But why, in nature, one colour should be preferred over another, I do not know. The berry is a plant's form of self-advertisement to encourage birds to eat it (however cross that may make us) so as to spread its progeny around. But why there should be wild differences in the colour selected, remains a mystery to me.

Black is by no means the commonest berry colouring, and yet it does occur in some very widespread instances. In common ivy, *Hedera helix*, for instance. Ivy berries ripen in February, when it is still winter, and birds (especially wood pigeons) go after them with relish. Privet (*Ligustrum*) berries are black and the heaviest-fruiting species in Britain are our native *L. vulgare* (commonest on alkaline soils) and the popular hedging species, *L. ovalifolium*. The fact that hedges have to be trimmed means that the latter species is seldom seen laden with fruit, but should you have the chance to cut branches of it in this condition, in October, and of combining them in an arrangement with the pink-and-orange fruit of spindle-berry, *Euonymus europaeus*, or some nearly related deciduous species or cultivar, you will be rather thrilled.

The best uses for black are in the most striking contrasts. There you have it, in black and white.

Alcea rosea 'Nigra'
Hollyhock
Height: 2m/7ft
Spread: 45cm/18in
Hardy, sun
A perennial with very dark maroon flowers that pass for black. Plant near to or at the front of a border so as to admire it at close quarters. Can be raised from seed or allowed to self-sow.

Anthriscus sylvestris 'Ravenswing'
Cow parsley
Height: 1m/40in
Spread: 45cm/18in
Hardy, partial shade
A short-lived perennial with lacy, dark purple foliage and stems, verging on black. Airy heads of white or light pink flowers appear in late spring. The foliage dies back around mid summer. Plant it with pink flowers. ▼

Dracunculus vulgaris
Dragon arum
Height: 60cm/2ft
Spread: 45cm/18in
Hardy, partial shade
A wicked-looking aroid, with glossy leaves and a dark purple-black spathe enclosing a jet-black club. The flower lasts for three days and, on first opening, smells of rotting meat and attracts blowflies to pollinate it. A born soloist.

Fatsia japonica
Japanese fatsia
Height: 3.5m/12ft
Spread: 3.5m/12ft
Hardy, sun or light shade
Round black fruits on contrasting white stems are a winter bonus on this bold, evergreen shrub. All year, its large, glossy, fingered leaves illuminate dull corners. White flowers appear in November, followed by the bunches of berries (see page 176).

Iris chrysographes
Height: 50cm/20in
Spread: 8cm/3in
Hardy, sun or light shade
A slender, elegant iris for a damp situation, with astonishingly dark flowers with gold markings on them. In forms such as 'Black Beauty' and 'Black Knight', the colour is so dark as to be near black. Try with brightly coloured candelabra primula. ▼

Kirengeshoma palmata
Height: 1.2m/4ft
Spread: 75cm/30in
Hardy, partial shade
A handsome woodland plant with well-defined, black stems and leaf veins. These set off well both the pale yellow flowers and the pale green leaves. For contrast, try an adjacent planting of a scarlet-berried arum.

Ophiopogon planiscapus 'Nigrescens'
Black lilyturf
Height: 15cm/6in
Spread: 30cm/12in
Hardy, sun
A tufted plant with narrow strap-like leaves, a bit like black grass. It can be planted in paving cracks or interwoven with green fronds of the New Zealand fern, Blechnum penna-marina. ▼

Phyllostachys nigra
Black bamboo
Height: 4m/13ft
Spread: 3m/10ft
Hardy, sun or light shade
A clump-forming bamboo with arching stems that turn black as they age. In P.n. forma nigra the stems turn black when younger. Plant where the colour of the stems will be seen, perhaps where the sun might strike it in the evening. ▼

Ranunculus ficaria 'Brazen Hussy'
Lesser celandine
Height: 10cm/4in
Spread: 15cm/6in
Hardy, sun
Bronze-black leaves and bright, shiny yellow flowers that open in the late winter and early spring sunshine; the whole plant retires out of sight below ground by the early summer. Plant in sun, otherwise the leaves will not be dark. ◄

Rhodochiton atrosanguineus
Height: 3m/10ft
Tender, sun
A black tubular corolla, with white anthers, adds drama to this annual climber's garlands of purple lampshades. Sow in the autumn, bring on under glass and plant out in the spring where it can clamber through winter jasmine or any other shrub.

Scabiosa atropurpurea 'Ace of Spades'
Pincushion flower
Height: 90cm/36in
Spread: 30cm/12in
Hardy, sun
Almost black flowers, accentuated by the white anthers which float above the dark petals. Plant amongst short, soft grasses.

Viola x wittrockiana ►
'T&M's Black Pansy'
Height: 10cm/4in
Spread: 10cm/4in
Hardy, short-lived perennial, best in sun
Many named pansies and violas of dubious origin have near-black flowers, coming more or less true from self-sown seedlings. They show up best against pale yellowish gravel.

INDEX

Page numbers in *italics* refer to the illustrations and captions.

Papaver 'Goliath'

AUTHOR'S ACKNOWLEDGEMENTS

Especial thanks to Jonathan Buckley, who has so devotedly been photographing my garden throughout the year since 1994. He is amazingly responsive to urgent summonses. We have also drawn on pictures he has taken elsewhere, though this was necessary in only a few cases. Erica Hunningher has been the most meticulous and devoted editor imaginable, and without ever becoming bossy, as is usually the downside of many conscientious editors. I must also thank Viv Bowler, my commissioning editor for the BBC, who has shown encouraging confidence in my book from the start. Let's hope it was justified.

The originator of the idea that I should write on the theme of Colour was Tom Cooper, my friend in Boston, Mass., under whose editorship I have written many pieces for publication in the American magazine *Horticulture*.

PHOTOGRAPHER'S ACKNOWLEDGEMENTS

It has been my privilege to visit Dixter regularly over the years throughout the seasons and, as I round the last bend in the lane and glimpse the house, my pulse never fails to quicken in anticipation of the latest excitements. The extraordinary magic of the place has as much to do with the people as with the garden and I would like to thank not only Christopher but also all the gardeners who have made me so welcome there. Both Erica and I are especially grateful to Fergus Garrett. His enthusiasm, encouragement and dedication have had an impact on this book which extends far beyond his own modest description of himself as simply a gardener.

All photographs were taken at Great Dixter, except those on the pages listed below
(*l* = left, *r* = right, *t* = top, *b* = bottom)
Beth Chatto Gardens, Elmstead Market, Essex, Beth Chatto, 33, 34*tl*, 45, 60*t*, 74*b*, 110, 111, 120*t*, 145*b*, 150*t*, 152*b*, 178*t*
Craigieburn, Dumfrieshire, Bill Chudziak, 67*t*
The Dingle, Powys, Roy and Barbara Joseph, 175*b*
Frenich, Perthshire, Colin Hamilton and Kulgin Dural, 51
The Garden House, Gloucestershire, Pam Schwerdt and Sibylle Kreutzberger, 74*t*, 99*t*, 106*tr*, 114*b*
Glen Chantry, Essex, Wol and Sue Staines, 55*tl*, 69, 187*tr*
Hergest Croft, Herefordshire, W.L. and R.A. Banks, 175*t*
Hollington Herb Garden, Berkshire, Judith and Simon Hopkinson, 59*b*
Ketley's, East Sussex, Helen Yemm, 76*b*
Miserden Nursery, Gloucestershire, Dave Robb, 63
The Old Vicarage, East Ruston, Norfolk, Alan Gray and Graham Robeson, 6, 29*l*, 71, 116,137*t* and *b*, 161*b*
Perch Hill Farm, East Sussex, Sarah Raven, 12*t*, 24*bl*, 36, 38*t* and *b*, 39, 66*b*, 77*bl*, 107*tl*, 183*b*, 187*tl* and *br*
RHS Gardens, Wisley, 94, 126*b*, 128*t*
Ruth Salisbury's garden, Gloucestershire, 4-5, 157*t*
Upper Mill Cottage, Kent, David and Mavis Seeney, 12*b*, 13*bl*, 26*b*, 29*r*, 35*tl*, 50*b*, 67*b*, 164*l*, 165*l*
West Dean Gardens, West Sussex, The Edward James Foundation, 156
White House Farm, Kent, Maurice Foster, 60*b* © Fergus Garrett